Praise for Using Formative Assessment to Differentiate Mathematics Instruction, Grades 4–10

"In this practical and thought-provoking book, Leslie Laud gives classroom teachers the tools they need to make formative assessment a reality. The book provides clear examples and compelling evidence to support assessment as a strategy to improve teaching and learning. The numerous self-assessments remind the reader that the best formative assessments are not merely given "to" students but are an interactive learning experience involving students, teachers, and professional colleagues. Best of all, the author offers time-saving strategies essential for every teacher in every discipline."

Douglas B. Reeves, Founder, The Leadership and Learning Center

"Leslie Laud shows the importance of the link between formative assessment and differentiated instruction. There is a limited body of work that combines these two constructs, and that connection makes this book powerful."

William Farber, Professor of Mathematics Education
Mercy College, Dobbs Ferry, NY

"Leslie Laud has created a very readable and comprehensive guide to understanding what formative assessment is and how to use it to meet the needs of students in the mathematics classroom. She offers many specific examples, covering a variety of approaches teachers can use. What is particularly noteworthy is her recognition that different teachers need to come at this work in different ways—that differentiating instruction is not just for students, but for teachers, too."

Marian Small, Author and Professional Development Consultant
One, Two . . . Infinity, New Brunswick, Canada

"Leslie Laud provides practical applications in mathematics assessment and instruction. She uses many vignettes and examples to paint a picture seen in many classrooms today. Throughout the book, Laud includes little gems that help with such areas as motivational strategies to self-determinism to ideas for visual representations. The many teacher tips and sound solutions will support those who are implementing RTI in mathematics."

Brad Witzel, Associate Professor of Special Education
Winthrop University, Rock Hill, SC

"Leslie Laud's book provides an invaluable road-map for mathematics teachers to understand what students are learning, to use this to systematically inform their instruction to better meet their students' needs, and to involve students more in their own learning. Each of these three elements can make a difference to student learning. Together, they have the power to transform what happens in our classrooms."

From the Foreword by Dylan Wiliam
Emeritus Professor of Educational Assessment
Institute of Education, University of London

"Many seemingly abstruse or vague concepts—such as differentiated instruction—come alive in the numerous vignettes . . . We see, for instance, numerous examples of ways to quickly assess relevant student background knowledge before teaching a new topic and how to use this information for tiered instruction following an RTI (Response to Intervention) model . . . Leslie Laud's attention to practical application makes this book a great tool to use for teacher study groups, and for mentoring those new to teaching—or new to teaching at a given grade level."

From the Foreword by Russell Gersten, Director
Instructional Research Group & Professor Emeritus
College of Education, University of Oregon

What Teachers Have to Say:

"Using Formative Assessment to Differentiate Mathematics Instruction provides teachers with a variety of options that they can put in place right away, with little disruption of what they currently do. The author provides many templates for students and teachers to use immediately, and makes a solid argument, based on research, that differentiation is an important component in student achievement."

Jeff Chaffee, Mathematics Curriculum
Enhancement Teacher
Remington Middle School, Franklin, MA

"I learned a great deal and plan to make some changes in my seventh grade math classroom. Leslie Laud takes the "fear" out of trying this method—she uses concrete examples that can be easily implemented in full or part by busy teachers. Her book gave me the initiative, reasons, and strategies to experiment with using formative assessments to drive tiered instruction in my classroom!"

Paul Kuhlman, Science and Seventh-Grade Math Teacher
Avon School District 4–1, Avon, SD

"In a world where time is always a concern, I appreciated the ready-to-teach tiered lesson examples and all of the resources that were shared. This book does a nice job of offering helpful websites and applicable resources to support the classroom teacher."

Rebecca Link, Middle School Math Teacher
Fort Recovery Middle School, Fort Recovery, OH

USING Formative Assessment to Differentiate Mathematics Instruction

GRADES 4–10

Seven Practices to Maximize Learning

LESLIE LAUD

A Joint Publication

CORWIN

NCTM | NATIONAL COUNCIL OF TEACHERS OF MATHEMATICS

CORWIN
A SAGE Company

FOR INFORMATION:

Corwin
A SAGE Company
2455 Teller Road
Thousand Oaks, California 91320
(800) 233-9936
Fax: (800) 417-2466
www.corwin.com

SAGE Ltd.
1 Oliver's Yard
55 City Road
London EC1Y 1SP
United Kingdom

SAGE India Pvt. Ltd.
B 1/I 1 Mohan Cooperative
Industrial Area
Mathura Road, New Delhi 110 044
India

SAGE Asia-Pacific Pte. Ltd.
33 Pekin Street #02-01
Far East Square
Singapore 048763

Acquisitions Editor: Carol Chambers Collins
Associate Editor: Megan Bedell
Editorial Assistant: Sarah Bartlett
Production Editor: Amy Schroller
Copy Editor: Amy Rosenstein
Typesetter: C&M Digitals (P) Ltd.
Proofreader: Charlotte Waisner
Indexer: Judy Hunt
Cover Designer: Michael Dubowe
Permissions Editor: Adele Hutchinson

Copyright © 2011 by Corwin

Printed in the United States of America

Library of Congress Cataloging-in-Publication Data

Laud, Leslie.
Using formative assessment to differentiate mathematics instruction, grades 4-10 : seven practices to maximize learning / Leslie Laud.

p. cm.
"A Joint Publication with National Council of Teachers of Mathematics."
Includes bibliographical references and index.

ISBN 978-1-4129-9524-5 (pbk. : alk. paper)

1. Mathematics—Study and teaching (Middle school)
2. Mathematics—Study and teaching (Secondary)
3. Curriculum planning. 4. Curriculum evaluation.
I. National Council of Teachers of Mathematics.
II. Title.

QA11.2.L38 2011 510.71'2—dc22 2011001911

This book is printed on acid-free paper.

NCTM Stock Number 14175

11 12 13 14 15 10 9 8 7 6 5 4 3 2 1

Contents

List of Figures

Chapter 4. Supporting Students Who Are Low Achieving

Chapter 5. Challenging Students Who Are High Achieving

Chapter 6. Time-Saving Management Strategies

Foreword

From Russell Gersten

Ongoing assessment of student learning in mathematics is far from easy, but it is certainly feasible. In mathematics, we can ask students to solve problems, explicitly show us or tell us or write down for us their strategy for solution. At the very least, we can quickly assess whether their answer is right or wrong, or at least partially correct. When time permits, we can also evaluate the level of understanding revealed in their choice of solution strategy.

There is a good deal of writing and rhetoric about using data for instructional decision-making. When the National Mathematics Panel, on which I served, reviewed the research literature on use of formative assessment, we found that when teachers regularly conducted formative assessment of student progress, students' growth in mathematics was accelerated significantly. We also found that this increase doubled when researchers provided teachers with specific techniques for using the data to reshape instruction.

Yet, at the current point in time, few such tools exist. Most guidelines are vague, idealistic and not always feasible for day-to-day use. Thus, the need for a volume such as the current one. Many seemingly abstruse or vague concepts—such as differentiated instruction—come alive in the numerous vignettes.

We see, for example, how to provide specific feedback that is constructive to students with disabilities in the regular mathematics classroom. We see numerous models of how to provide sensible, differentiated instruction for this group of students as well as others who are struggling. We see numerous examples of ways to quickly assess relevant student background knowledge before teaching a new topic and how to use this information for tiered instruction following an RTI (Response to Intervention) model.

The author reminds us of the relevance of some of the older research from the 1960s and 1970s, again by providing examples of how distributed practice makes instruction so much more interesting and powerful than the typical habit of massed practice with no cumulative review. We also see a creative use of the powerful summarization strategy– perhaps the major contribution of this book.

This volume helps demystify concepts that are often vague and amorphous; the author's attention to practical application makes it a great tool to use for teacher study groups, and for mentoring those new to teaching—or new to teaching at a given grade level.

Russell Gersten
Director, Instructional Research Group & Professor Emeritus
College of Education, University of Oregon

From Dylan Wiliam

Students do not learn what we teach. We plan our lessons with great care, students seem to be engaged in what we are doing (most of the time), but yet, when we take in their notebooks, what they have learned often seems to bear little or no relation to what we have taught. Anyone who has spent any time in a classroom knows this; no matter how well designed the instruction is, it is impossible to predict with any certainty what students will learn as a result. This is why assessment is the central process in effective instruction. Assessment is the bridge between teaching and learning. It is only by assessing where students are that we can make smart decisions about what to do next.

Many years ago, David Ausubel suggested that the most important factor influencing learning is what the learner already knows, and that teachers should ascertain this, and teach accordingly. Almost half a century later, we are just beginning to realize how difficult it is to put this simple-sounding advice into practice. Sure, we can find out where the learners are at the beginning of a sequence of instruction, but even if all the learners in a class are at the same place when the lesson starts (highly unlikely!), within minutes, students will have reached different understandings.

From this perspective, integrating assessment with instruction sounds impossibly complex. Fortunately, help is at hand. In this very readable book, Leslie Laud shares with us her experiences of working with teachers in real classrooms who have begun the task of trying to make their teaching more responsive to their students' needs.

This book is at the same time well grounded in the latest research evidence, and very practical. It contains a number of templates that can be immediately used in mathematics classrooms, or modified to accommodate differences in teaching style. More unusually, it is not just a list of smart-sounding ideas dreamed up in an office, but incorporates many real-life examples from teachers who are developing their own use of classroom assessment to improve their teaching. The book is also realistic, in that it recognizes how little spare time teachers have for innovation, and provides a number of concrete starting points for teachers, either working alone, or in teams.

In short, Laud's book provides an invaluable road-map for mathematics teachers to understand what students are learning, to use this to systematically inform their instruction to better meet their students' needs, and to involve students more in their own learning. Each of these three elements can make a difference to student learning. Together, they have the power to transform what happens in our classrooms.

Dylan Wiliam, Emeritus Professor of Educational Assessment
Institute of Education, University of London

Preface

"But for tiny adjustments, if we knew how to make them, we could release the genius in every child."

—Albert Einstein (cited in Murray & Jorgensen, 2007)

As a teacher committed to implementing the principles of the National Council of Teachers of Mathematics (NCTM) and therefore using formative assessment to differentiate instruction in my classroom, I sought guidance on the practical issues that arise and a coherent description of what exactly these principles would look like in actual exemplary classrooms. But I did not find enough. After developing my own resources and formulating a theoretical and practical framework for how to use formative assessment to differentiate instruction in mathematics, I found an overwhelming demand among other math teachers at conferences, in math education courses I teach, and in schools where I consult to learn more about how they can do this effectively in their own classrooms.

The NCTM (2000) strongly recommends, in its first and arguably most important principle—the Equity Principle—that all students receive challenging math instruction, support, and enrichment. This book provides a road map for using formative assessment to differentiate instruction, most specifically in Chapter 2, making achieving the equity principle more within the reach of teachers. Furthermore, the assessment strategies I describe are aligned with the NCTM's recommendations that assessment be an integral part of instruction used regularly to inform decision-making.

A growing research base shows that instruction is most effective when differentiated so that students are taught at their individual instructional levels (Heubner, 2010). When instruction is either too difficult or too easy, students become frustrated or bored, and learning declines. When teachers use formative assessment to understand where students are in their learning, then differentiated instruction is more effective. Although there is growing substantial research on the effectiveness of differentiating instruction, not many large-scale studies have been conducted. In contrast, researchers have collected more than 250 articles and book chapters, all showing the tremendous effectiveness of formative assessment on raising student achievement (Black & Wiliam, 1998). Given the strength of the research base on formative assessment, which meets the requirements of legislation such as No Child Left Behind and Response to Intervention that require schools to use research-based methods, there has been a turn to formative assessment and differentiating instruction to improve how math is taught.

This book cites seminal and recent research and describes the instructional procedures found effective for teaching middle school mathematics through a unique comprehensive framework of seven practices that I have assembled, based on research and my classroom experiences. This book's content was tested, reviewed, and enhanced in more than 70 hours of meeting time by experienced math teachers. The author met with these teachers weekly in 2-hour blocks after school to share ideas, listen to their ideas, and coplan strategies to test in the classroom. Then, in an action research format, the teachers tested them out with real classes of students and reflected on the results. Woven throughout the book are practical teacher-tested suggestions, real-world examples, and student activities, followed by a list of recommended resources at the end.

Teachers are busy. That is why I include reproducible handouts of exercises and activities that can be used immediately with students. The suggestions can be used step by step, all designed with time management in mind. As most mathematics teachers are bound by school requirements that they teach a prescribed curriculum (one of several challenges mathematics educators face), this book offers a format for how teachers can adapt existing lessons from the texts they must use to deliver them in a more differentiated way. Not only teachers working in heterogeneously grouped classrooms can benefit from differentiating in these ways, but even in homogenously grouped classrooms, teachers acknowledge that there is still a wide array of abilities and diverse approaches to learning.

Chapter 1 opens with vignettes of three teachers using formative assessment to differentiate instruction in individualized ways. Then readers are offered a self-assessment on differentiation and an introduction to the seven-practices framework. This provides teachers with an instant big picture snapshot of what a differentiated math class looks like as well as concise directions for how to work toward achieving this. Research on the benefits of differentiated instruction and formative assessment are presented in this chapter as well as suggestions for creating a class climate or norms in which students work independently and appreciate that they may need to do different work, given that we all have unique learning styles and needs.

Assessment as the core of differentiated instruction is addressed in Chapter 2. Diagnostic preassessments and strategies for collecting formative assessment data on a regular basis are discussed in depth. An array of preassessment options is presented as well as suggestions for continuous formative assessment. A comprehensive picture of how to use these data is given, followed by a discussion of the importance of students' self-scoring assessments and using the data to inform next steps they will take in their learning. As most teachers may be responsible for more than a hundred or more students by middle school, the most practical and time-efficient ways to create, adapt, collect, and analyze these assessments are suggested. The chapter concludes with cautions on how assessment can impact confidence and motivation, followed by recommendations for how to make this more positive.

In Chapter 3, an overview of tiered unit and lesson planning is provided along with five model-tiered lessons, with formats for lesson planning and reproducible handouts for students. Tiering is broadly discussed in terms of how teachers can naturally and easily tier lessons regularly. Also emphasized are making assignments equally interesting for all students and not assigning more or less work to different groups.

Chapter 4 addresses specific strategies for supporting low-achieving math students. If after using the strategies suggested in Chapters 1–3, some students still struggle, then Chapter 4 offers a broad framework for fine tuning differentiation supports. Research-validated strategies are presented to address basic fact gaps, conceptual understanding challenges, and procedural calculation difficulties.

Chapter 5 addresses techniques for challenging students who are math talented. It offers suggestions for how to design open-ended, abstract, and complex tasks and enrichments within lessons or during class discussions. Fundamental modifications, such as curriculum compacting and creating learning contracts, are presented, along with practical examples and reproducibles. Models of effective higher order questioning strategies as well as instant challenge templates for pushing students to clarify and extend thinking are also presented.

Chapter 6 provides time-management strategies for running a differentiated classroom, including unit planning, grouping and managing students working on different tasks, assigning and correcting homework, and grading.

The following chapters represent a journey that I took in my own classroom, with colleagues in the schools in which I have worked, the teachers who have taken my courses, and the teachers in the small groups that I have led. It has been a privilege to learn from these talented people. It is my hope that your journey through these pages, and the experiences you will gain from testing out these strategies in your own classrooms, will be as rewarding for you and your students' learning as it has been for us.

Acknowledgments

I would like to acknowledge everyone at Corwin who has helped along the way, especially my editor Carol Collins. I thank Chris Muller, director of the American International School of Lusaka, for inspiring my interest in this topic, and Tony Brown, United Nations International School (UNIS) Middle School Principal, for supporting this interest. I owe gratitude to the math teachers at UNIS for all I learned from them. I also thank those who took my courses on differentiating mathematics, particularly Jackie Tchang for her feedback on a draft. The teachers at Wellesley Middle School deserve far more than an acknowledgment. Nancy Cali, Mathematics Department Head, gave me the opportunity to work with the math teachers, along with her support and encouragement. Marty Wagner and Susan Hirsch provided detailed feedback on every chapter, invaluable ideas, and served as the inspiration behind most of the anecdotes. Julie Fila and Laura Palin then joined the group and made invaluable contributions as well. Ideas taken from the excellent mathematics teaching my son received at Wellesley Middle School are peppered throughout. Finally, I cannot thank my family enough for their support and allowing me the time to work on this project, particularly my son Arjun.

Publisher's Acknowledgments

Corwin gratefully acknowledges the contributions of the following reviewers:

Jeff Chaffee, Mathematics Curriculum Enhancement Teacher
Remington Middle School
Franklin, MA

William Farber, Professor of Mathematics Education
Mercy College
Dobbs Ferry, NY

Melva R. Grant, Faculty
Old Dominion University
Darden College of Education
Department of STEM Education and Professional Studies
Norfolk, VA

Karen Hyers, Senior High Mathematics Teacher and District Curriculum
  Coordinator
Tartan High School
ISD 622: North St. Paul-Maplewood-Oakdale Schools
Oakdale, MN

Steve Isaak, Eleventh- and Twelfth-Grade Math Teacher
Advanced Technologies Academy
Las Vegas, NV

Paul Kuhlman, Science Teacher and Seventh-Grade Math Teacher
Avon School District 4–1
Avon, SD

Becky Link, Math Teacher
Fort Recovery Middle School
Fort Recovery, OH

Laura F. Main, Math Specialist and Doctoral Candidate in Instructional
  Leadership
New Canaan Public Schools and Western Connecticut State University
New Canaan, CT, and Danbury, CT

Diane K. Masarik, Assistant Professor
University of Wisconsin, Eau Claire
Mathematics Department
Eau Claire, WI

Ann Wallace, Secondary Math Education Advisor
James Madison University
College of Education
Harrisonburg, VA

LeAnne Yenny, Seventh-Grade Math and Science Teacher
Bozeman School District 7
Bozeman, MT

About the Author

 **Leslie Laud, EdD,** has differentiated math instruction in her own classroom and in her coteaching with her math colleagues, and has been doing so for almost two decades. She teaches an online course on Differentiated Middle School Math Instruction at Bank Street College of Education. In addition, she has presented at many conferences both nationally and internationally, including The National Council of Teachers of Mathematics annual conference. She has also published many articles in leading journals such as *Educational Leadership* and *Teaching Exceptional Children.* She currently leads staff development groups with teachers in school systems in the Boston area. She received both her doctorate in curriculum and instruction and her master's in special education from Teachers College, Columbia University.

To Kishor, Arjun, and Ravi

1

Getting Started and Establishing Norms

In the following vignettes, these teachers choose to enhance how they use formative assessment data to differentiate instruction in alternative ways. They all begin in different places and pursue individualized goals.

Ms. Chou decided to enhance how she used formative assessment to differentiate instruction after first identifying practices she already used, such as giving differentiated homework assignments and tests. She decided her next step would be giving diagnostic preassessments before units. Though she usually knew where her students were, a colleague reminded her that preassessments also benefit the students when they self-correct them and get an idea of what they need to work on. As an example, on a trial preassessment, one typically high-achieving student only scored 12/15, which surprised Ms. Chou. She had assumed that he had already mastered these skills and was planning to give him and several others an enrichment investigation task. Instead, she now chose to wait and shore up the skills he had missed. She was thrilled to hear him explain, "I missed the questions on volume of prisms and cylinders. It must have been due to calculation errors because I know the formulas. I found several model problems in a supplementary text. I'm going to practice these two types again and see if I can get the calculations right." In addition to her now knowing where to focus her teaching, the student also now knew exactly where he needed to focus his learning.

In contrast, Mr. Martin decided to begin with smaller formative assessment check-ins. He chose to begin with check-ins so that he could monitor how students were doing throughout the unit. After reviewing the class's homework and finding two minor error patterns, he designed a quick check-in task during a unit on solving linear equations. He had students solve two linear equations and substitute the solution

1

back into the original equations as a way of teaching his students how to self-check their work. He then reviewed the activity with the class, pointed out all they seemed to understand well, and then helped his students use the check-in to identify which of the two different types of errors they were making. He reviewed each type, then had them select which further practice to do based on which type of error they had made.

Ms. Musambee had been giving preassessments for some time and wanted to enhance how she handled the subsequent forming of groups. In the past, she had often created three groups based on those who knew most of the material, some, or had no prior learning of it. Instead, she wanted to do a deeper error analysis and group students according to their specific inclinations and conceptual misunderstandings. She also wanted to move beyond just grouping by readiness levels so that she could strengthen the class norm that "we all learn differently" and move away from students regularly comparing each other hierarchically. To do this, she redesigned her preassessment to better capture these different conceptual understandings and to include a more substantial self-reflective evaluation for students to complete. They were able to more closely analyze their strengths as well as the kinds of conceptual errors they made and understand why they may have made them. The students proved adept and thoughtful in their analyses of their preassessments. Ms. Musambee then used this more complex, detailed information to form more nuanced groupings. She found four different tasks that allowed them to begin practicing strategies for addressing the specific conceptual understandings, ranging from those who inverted the first fraction when dividing to those who needed to refine how precisely they could explain why the second is inverted.

GETTING STARTED

These three teachers understand that achieving a comprehensive vision of using formative assessment to differentiate instruction is achieved slowly over time, and each teacher's path to doing so is unique. Identifying where you already are can prove helpful toward deciding how to enhance your use of formative assessment to differentiate math instruction. This process can begin with completing the self-assessment shown in Figure 1.1. You can then see what you already do and choose next steps to take.

Formative assessment has been defined as teachers or students using data as a basis for decisions about next steps to take toward achieving learning goals, and to then make instructional decisions that are better than those that would have been made without this data (Wiliam, 2010). When using formative assessment, differentiation is the natural next step. Carol Ann Tomlinson (1999) has defined differentiating instruction as an organized, flexible, and proactive approach to adjusting instruction so that it best meets the needs of all learners and promotes maximum growth for all. Aiming to achieve this goal is a core of *equity*, which is the first of the six principles of high-quality mathematics education recommended by the National Council of Teachers of Mathematics (2000).

In a comprehensive approach to using formative assessment to differentiate math instruction, teachers would work toward regularly using the following seven practices. I developed this group of practices to help guide the teachers that I have worked with on using formative

Figure 1.1

Teacher Self-Assessment

Differentiating Math Practices Rubric

We all begin in different places and pursue different goals as we grow as teachers. This self-assessment provides an overview of practices that can enhance your skills at using formative assessment to differentiate instruction, rather than a required to-do list.

On a scale of 1–4, rate how frequently you do each practice:

1—I do this often,　　　　2—occasionally,　　　　3—have tried it,　　　　4—haven't tried this yet

Convey Norms and Targets

I foster self-directed, independent approaches to learning.	1	2	3	4
I emphasize to students that doing different work helps everyone get what he or she needs.	1	2	3	4
I clearly convey objectives (targets) before each unit.	1	2	3	4

Assessment

I use diagnostic preassessment tasks before each unit.	1	2	3	4
I systematically collect informal and formal assessment data all along.	1	2	3	4

Coplan Next Steps

I use assessment data to tier homework, class activities, and assessments.	1	2	3	4
I have students self-score assessments and use the results to decide next steps to take.	1	2	3	4
I stress the importance of self-initiated student learning, based on teacher feedback and self-scored assessments.	1	2	3	4

Grouping and Tiering

I regularly use flexible groupings (often 3) for differentiated tasks.	1	2	3	4
Based on my review of homework and /or class participation during instruction, I enable those students who indicate mastery to move on as I assist others.	1	2	3	4
I draw on supplemental resources (alternate texts/websites) for differentiated activities.	1	2	3	4

Challenge and Support

I select from my own bank of strategies for filling in calculation gaps, solidifying procedural steps, and clarifying concepts.	1	2	3	4
I select from my own bank of strategies for challenging students such as open-ended tasks, higher order questions, abstract project, projects compacting contracts, and extension resources.	1	2	3	4

Homework and Graded Assessments

I differentiate homework and assessments and hold students accountable for the different work they do.	1	2	3	4

assessment to differentiate math instruction. Most are drawn from research-based principles, while others that emphasize application of these principles emerged from our conversations.

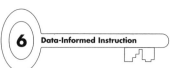

1. Build supportive and self-directive class climate norms (Andrade, 2010).

2. Clarify learning targets and convey them (Wiliam, 2010).

3. Preassess before each topic and continuously engineer discussions, activities and tasks all along that are purposefully designed to elicit specific student understandings (Wiliam, 2010).

4. Involve students in using assessment data and teacher feedback to inform next steps they will take in their learning (Wiliam, 2010).

5. Use assessment data to group students for differentiated activities via centers, varied tasks, projects, performances, and presentations (Tieso, 2005).

6. Use assessment data to further challenge and support all learners.

7. Differentiate homework and graded assessments.

As a caveat, and this reminder will continue to be stressed throughout the book, this list is not something that teachers should expect to adopt quickly or fully. When teachers I worked with tested out these practices, they used different practices and quickly discovered that student achievement rose in notable and exciting ways when they only used a few of the practices, and even those only partially. They repeatedly recommended that I emphasize this. The practices are not an exhaustive list, but a buffet. Even choosing and using only a few will uplift student achievement.

How do these practices fit into a
Response to Intervention (RTI) model?

1. Select research-based Tier I instructional program.

   Since the basis of these practices, formative assessment, is research-based, it meets RTI requirements

2. Collect assessment data.

These can include state assessment results, internally developed assessments, universal screening probes, and other sources described in Chapter 2.

3. Use data to differentiate Tier I instruction and to ensure 80% of students are thriving in Tier I.

Chapter 3 describes differentiation methods.

4. Analyze data to determine students to receive Tier II interventions.

5. Provide interventions via small groups in class or outside of class (before or after school, study hall).

Chapter 4 details specific interventions.

6. Collect additional progress-monitoring data weekly on students receiving Tier II interventions.

Chapter 2 overviews progress monitoring.

For a comprehensive overview of RTI and math, see Riccomini & Witzel (2010b).

The seven practices can also be understood in terms of what actions might be considered as exemplifying formative assessment and differentiated instruction and which would not, as the following chart shows. I created this chart to help teachers more readily see the distinctions between these two types of models. It is modeled after similar charts presented by differentiation experts such as Heacox (2002).

The Differentiated Classroom	The Traditional Classroom
Practice 1:	
• Teacher consciously cultivates a supportive climate	• Competitive climate flourishes
Practice 2:	
• Unit targets conveyed up front	• Targets not conveyed, or only just before tests
Practice 3:	
• Preassessment precedes each unit • Engineered discussions, tasks, and activities are used to elicit specified insights into student understandings (Wiliam, 2010)	• Only summative tests used • Insights into student understandings are unplanned and incidental

(Continued)

(Continued)

The Differentiated Classroom	The Traditional Classroom
Practice 4:	
• Teachers assess, and students self-assess, what's understood constantly, and this drives teaching and learning • Each student helped to get what he or she needs	• Curriculum or text drives what is taught • Same work for all
Practice 5:	
• Lessons break off into tiers • Frequent and flexible groupings	• Whole class usually instructed together
Practice 6:	
• Student-centered supports and challenges	• Teacher/text centered
Practice 7:	
• Differentiated homework and tests, and grading systems	• Same homework and unit tests for all

Again, these practices can seem daunting. As mentioned at the start, teachers need to pursue how they will implement these kinds of practices in individualized ways and at different paces, beginning by noting those they already do, then weighing the need for each, prioritizing and selecting which to focus on each year. The preassessment (Figure 1.1) can serve as a guide in this process.

The rest of this book takes up Practices 2–7 in detail. However, the second section of this chapter focuses on Practice 1, setting norms. The teachers I have worked with have consistently given establishing class norms top priority.

ESTABLISHING CLASS NORMS

On the fourth day of school, Mr. Miles has his students break into cooperative learning groups to work on a data-analysis project. He created this project based on interests they expressed when they completed a survey on ways they spend their recreation time. In class, Mr. Miles explains each of the four data-analysis tasks. Each student then moves to one of four tables with others who have selected the same task.

Once seated, the students are given the task of plotting the data for how their group members spend their recreation time on a box-and-whiskers diagram, yet done in one of four ways. Mr. Miles allows them to choose whether they want to:

1. *Use lists to explain why they set up the box-and-whiskers diagram as they did.*

2. *Create a flow chart to explain why they did it as they did.*

3. *Act out the chart physically by standing where each quartile would be drawn on a life-sized graph.*

4. *Create an alternate diagram to convey the same information.*

Because he had earlier asked the class for a show of hands if anyone had familiarity with this model and no hands went up, this "instant formative assessment" enabled him to know that differentiating by readiness levels was not possible. However, he did expect that some students would master the topic at a quicker pace, and so he had built a challenge into the end of the activity to differentiate according to their needs. After they completed the tasks, he had them reflect on the lesson, beginning some conversations that would continue all year. He has found that every year some students announce that they are "bad at math." He chose to open up this conversation today because this task had a broad array of math in it and students could use it to break down this notion. They could see that while some elements of math might be difficult, such as arranging the data accurately or doing certain calculations with the data, there might be other aspects such as designing a visual model that are a breeze for certain students. Mr. Miles also had them reflect on how they each learned the task and raised another point that he will reinforce all year that "we all learn differently." An implicit message he begins to send less directly is that different approaches and paces will be valued and respected. He does this primarily through modeling it. He purposely calls on Tim, a student known by his peers to be struggling in math, to explain to the class why outliers are not included in the plotted quantities. He was pleased when he had circulated among the groups during the project to see that Tim, who is so strong visually, had instantly seen why this is the case. Since Tim has a language-based, diagnosed disability, Mr. Miles spent a few moments supporting Tim's efforts to explain the idea behind this concept to his peers in the group. Instead of telling him "great job," he had given Tim some advice on how to explain his reasoning more clearly to the group, then to the class. Tim was clearly intrinsically satisfied and proud of his achievement. Mr. Miles was careful to focus on pointing out Tim's use of his visual abilities so that he might remember to utilize this skill regularly. Mr. Miles also focused on complimenting Tim's efforts, rather than his achievement, as research has found this focus uplifts motivation and achievement (Hattie & Timperley, 2007).

Mr. Miles conveys an expectation that all students will value learning differences, making everyone feel safe no matter how they learn. "Since we are all individuals who learn differently, different learning experiences are to be expected, and so you will often do different tasks to achieve the same learning," he explains. Knowing that the science department is currently teaching a unit on constants and variables, he reminds them that becoming more proficient with essential unit learnings should be a constant for every student, whereas how this is achieved will vary for each student.

Before assigning homework, he wraps up the lesson by asking students to share, after they have corrected a final practice task, whether their corrections show that they have "got it," "need more practice," or "have questions." He has learned through experience that students need to make this self-evaluation with data from a task that backs up their choice. For example, if they got 19/20 correct and easily answered questions in class, they can use this as an argument. However, if they only got half the answers correct and these were not simple errors, this would indicate that they "have questions." In the past when he had asked this, he would find many students would state they have "got it," then he would find at quiz time that they had not, particularly with struggling students who notoriously have difficulty with accurate self-assessment (Andrade, 2010). As self-assessment is a basis for becoming self-directed, a core norm he cultivates, he carefully designs repeated opportunities to coach students in developing these skills, through offering frequent practice, followed by feedback and guidance on their efforts.

As they each state where they are in their understanding of the topic, Mr. Miles is careful to remain nonjudgmental, avoiding complimenting students who did well. He has realized that privileging kids who perform well sends a message that can undermine establishing a climate in which all levels of performance are respected. Also he now believes the band of capability is narrower than he had thought earlier in his career. Over the years, he has seen many students excel with the right support and extended effort. Hence, he compliments perseverance and effort, which he has come to realize may be bigger factors in determining which students will excel.

As students ask clarifying questions about the homework he has assigned for that evening, he notes in their homework study books that a few should skip the main practice section and do only the final challenge problems. He again is careful not to convey a congratulatory tone, but rather just an observation when he makes this determination for certain students, based on how well they had shown mastery of the material in class and on the final wrap-up practice assessment task. In this way, he avoids making others who do require the extra practice to feel any less than those who skip ahead. "We all should seek ways to get what we need," he reminds them, "whether you do the practice or the challenge is not the central issue. What matters is whether, in the end, you master the targets for the unit."

When he recommends that one student do the practice problems and a few extra, he is careful to focus on the task and not on her as a person, as research has shown this is important to increasing achievement (Hattie & Timperley, 2007). "I see you got the first parts of the problem correct, which was ordering the data then averaging the middle data points. You yourself have made a note here that you need to practice plotting data some more. So I agree that it looks like you will master it if you practice a few more." To foster trust and encourage her, he points out what she did well and conveys that he believes she is close to mastering the task, emphasizing how hard she has worked and the effective processes she is using. Then, he gave her pointed feedback on what to focus on, specifically, and helped her gauge how much practice she will need to master the topic. After this quick homework clarification time, he dismisses his students.

In this snapshot, Mr. Miles is hard at work establishing important class norms that foster the kind of climate in which students feel supported, safe, and comfortable with differences. In addition, he carefully cultivates independent work habits and a self-directed approach to learning, which are necessary if students will be working on differentiated tasks in his class during the year and so will not have whole group instruction and direct teacher guidance at all times.

Model Respect for All

Supportive Classroom Climate **1**

Mr. Miles models respect for all students when he purposefully distributes his praise among all students, those who tackle problems creatively and those who draw on personal strengths, even when aspects of the math do not come easily for them. Again, he does not compliment student achievement as much as he compliments effort and specific approaches they have used so that they will be more aware of the effectiveness of these. For example, when Tim, a student with special needs, immediately grasped why outliers are not included in box-and-whisker graphs, Mr. Miles used this chance to hold up the student as an example before his peers. Mr. Miles is also careful not to overvalue "logico-mathematical" intelligence (Gardner, 1983) when he praises students. Instead, he carefully compliments students on factors that are more easily within their control, such as effort level. He does not use the phrase, "good job," but instead focuses on giving feedback on the task such as, "I saw you do 24 extra problems and then you remembered all the steps on the quiz we took the next day." In his many years of teaching, he has seen students who struggle in math make tremendous leaps with the right coaching and practice. So he has come to believe that all students can move forward in becoming more proficient with essential unit learnings when given the right conditions. If all students have more potential for capability than one might realize, he reasons, then praise should be used to build strategic approaches and effort in all.

Establish a Climate of Respecting Differences

Mr. Miles cultivates a respectful classroom climate in which it is expected that all students will respect their peers' unique learning profiles in ways that make everyone feel safe and supported. Rather than working to make differences invisible, he celebrates them from the start. He constantly points out how some learners may instantly "see" a concept but struggle with articulating it. Conversely, some can make lists easily that enable them to articulate an explanation of a concept. When students claim they are "bad" at math, he strives to undo that notion by having them break down and identify what aspects they struggle with, and how they can use their strengths to compensate. He is careful with the language students use when correcting work or use when they are unsure about a concept. He doesn't allow them to say "I don't know this." Instead, they say, "I haven't learned this yet" or "I have questions."

Mr. Miles emphasizes that since all students are different, giving the same work to all would unfairly privilege one learning profile over another. Differentiation is actually fairer because it acknowledges individual learning differences. He admits that even now, he still struggles with giving clearly more challenging work to some students without making others feel inadequate. He acknowledges that this is fair, yet it is something that is a struggle for many teachers I have known, and something that they have actively worked to address within themselves. When certain preassessments show vastly different readiness levels, putting students into leveled groups makes the most sense. Yet at this time, middle school and older students are highly adept at quickly determining "high" and "low" groups, and this cannot be easily minimized. However, Mr. Miles has seen so many cases where the "low" group, when given a chance to work up through properly leveled work, attains the same mastery of the standards as those who began at higher readiness levels (though they may not excel at all the challenges in the same way as those who spent time during the unit working on challenge activities). This evidence has made his own discomfort with giving leveled material decrease. He is more casual now when he discreetly forms groups, confident that he is taking the right measures to give each student what he or she needs to be able to come up to the standard level and to challenge those who began at the standard. He has also become more capable of designing preassessments that reveal more nuanced conceptual differences that he can use to form groups rather than forming them based only on readiness levels.

Cultivate Self-Directed Learning

1 Supportive Classroom Climate

The National Council of Teachers of Mathematics (2000) states that "students learn more and learn better when they take control of their learning by defining their goals and monitoring their progress" (p. 21). Self-directed learners, researchers have found, learn more and are more successful academically in school (Andrade, 2010). Introducing formative assessments, described in detail in Chapter 2, that students self-score, then use to design plans for how they will master concepts they have yet to learn, is a step toward becoming more self-directed. Cultivating such self direction requires teacher modeling, feedback, and ongoing coaching. When teachers I have worked with have strived to cultivate this kind of self-direction, they have been surprised by the extent of modeling, feed-back, and ongoing coaching that students require, and for some students their movement along the continuum of self-directedness is much slower than for others. Fostering a climate of self-directed learning informed by ongoing formative assessment is something that takes place from the moment students enter a room until they leave, as Mr. Miles demonstrates.

He begins to nurture self-directed learning with practices such as giving preassessments and having students self-score them, then use what they find from these to self-direct the next steps they will take. Essentially, he works to put his students in charge of understanding and managing how they will learn.

He constantly has them not only self-evaluate their learning of each topic with carefully selected phrases such as, "got it," "need more prac-tice," or "have questions," but he also then expects his students to make a plan for what they should do next to move ahead in their learning. He understands that while correcting one's work with an answer key is a simple self-assessment, reflecting on one's deeper understanding of a con-cept is more challenging, and so students require more coaching, practice, and modeling to hone this skill. Teacher time is limited, and so teachers must make a judgment call about how much time to invest in supporting students in this process. At times, it may be more time efficient to point out conceptual misunderstandings for students rather than scaffolding them in discovering these themselves. As well, some students may be more talented at learning how to do this for themselves, and it may need to be acknowledged that other students will continuously require more direction with doing this.

When students ask questions, he turns them around, and using questions, allows them to realize that they already do understand much of the concept and sometimes they can answer their own question with the right support. In this way, he encourages perseverance and avoids being seen as the sole math authority in a way that could diminish his students' belief in their own skills and abilities.

In these ways, particularly those described in Chapter 2, Mr. Miles builds a climate in his classroom in which students feel supported, safe, and comfortable and become self-directed in how they approach learning.

2

Formative Assessment

After giving her students 15 minutes to complete a first diagnostic preassessment of the year on addition and subtraction of fractions (see Figure 2.1), Ms. Musambee reassured them that she would not be grading it or even looking at it, unless they wanted her to do so. This activity was just for them to determine what they had learned about fractions in the past. It would be used only to help them find what they would need to work on to master these procedures in the upcoming unit. "Doing this pretest is designed to help each of you get what you need in the coming new unit," she explained. The results of the pretest would enable them to determine what next steps they needed to take individually and for her to see what differentiated adjustments she should make her instruction. She deliberately chose not to compel them to turn in this first preassessment of the year to her because part of her purpose was to help them feel comfortable with these and to convey that these preassessments have value that goes beyond her use of them. In the future, students invariably do show them to her.

Figure 2.1

Fractions Preassessment

Rate how well you feel you know how to do each on a scale of 1−4, with

1 = not so well   4 = very well

Add/subtract fractions with like denominators	1	2	3	4
Add/subtract fractions with unlike denominators	1	2	3	4
Add/subtract fractions with mixed numbers	1	2	3	4
Add/subtract fractions with re-grouping	1	2	3	4

Solve the following problems:

$\frac{1}{3} + \frac{1}{3}$ $\frac{3}{4} - \frac{1}{4}$

$\frac{1}{2} + \frac{1}{3}$ $\frac{3}{5} - \frac{1}{3}$

$1\frac{1}{2} - \frac{1}{4}$ $2\frac{4}{7} - 1\frac{3}{4}$

$2\frac{3}{4} - 1\frac{1}{2}$ $3\frac{1}{2} + 1\frac{3}{5}$

Stop here and wait for directions on self-correcting preassessment.

Analyze your corrections

Check error type you made for each problem: Simple*   Procedure**   Concept***

Add/subtract fractions with like denominators

Add/subtract fractions with unlike denominators

Add/subtract fractions with mixed numbers

Add/subtract fractions with a regrouping

*Simple = missed a basic fact or made a simple error that I immediately recognized

**Procedure = missed a step or did a step out of order

***Concept = applied the wrong procedure, a wrong step, or didn't know what to do

On the preassessment, students are first asked, using a scale of 1–4, to rate their comfort with performing each type of operation (addition, subtraction, regrouping, all with like/unlike denominators). Then the students are asked to solve four groups of problems that are presented in a sequence mirroring the order of the self-assessment rating statements at the top of the page. In this way, the preassessment clearly lists the unit's targets, and she points this out to them.

After the 15-minute period, Ms. Musambee posts the answer key on the Smart Board and directs her students to put their pencils away and to take out red pens to correct their work. Next, they analyze their errors using the guide at the bottom of the preassessment. Then they use evidence from their pretests to determine which operations they had already learned and which they need to learn. Her students then choose their class work and homework from a differentiated list of tiered or leveled options, depending on what they personally needed (see Figure 2.2). After engaging in the error analysis, they then have the choice of turning in the preassessment or saving it and writing a note to Ms. Musambee on what next steps they plan to take, based on what they learned about themselves from the preassessments. Earlier in the year, some chose to keep their preassessments to themselves the first time they took one. However, as trust grew over the year and her students came to value her feedback, they all passed them back to her to get her input.

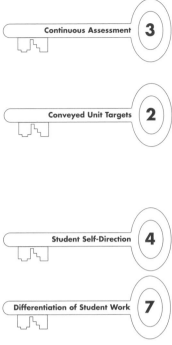

Continuous Assessment **3**

Conveyed Unit Targets **2**

Student Self-Direction **4**

Differentiation of Student Work **7**

Figure 2.2

Preassessment Homework Choices

Choice One

If you made errors that were primarily simple, do all problems on page __ in the text.

Choice Two

If you made errors that were primarily conceptual or procedural, do the examples and regular problems on page __ in the text.

Choice Three

If you made almost no errors, do the final four problems on page __ in the text and work on two challenge problems.

*If you like, you may also do the challenge problems no matter what choice you make.

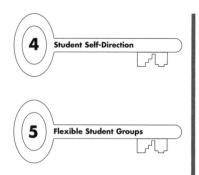

When Ms. Musambee had students select from the three choices in Figure 2.2, based on how they did on the preassessment, all those students who had chosen to show her preassessments (which was most of the class) made appropriate choices based on the error types they had made. Ms. Musambee was ready to offer guiding encouragement if any students chose options not matched to their readiness, though this was rarely needed. Students then moved into groups of "ones" at one table, and the other numbers went to other designated tables. Ms. Musambee then rotated from table to table offering assistance. Those who made errors were to compare their error analyses with similar errors made on other work they had done. This is difficult work, even for teachers. Students need modeling, practice, and coaching to learn to do this effectively, which she provided before that lesson and would continue to provide. They would do so in a format such as that shown in Figure 2.3.

Figure 2.3

Determining My Next Steps

Copy several sample errors and defend why you feel your errors were primarily simple, procedural, or conceptual.

My errors are often **simple,** so I will:

- Work more slowly.
- Check my work at the end by redoing simple calculations.
- Put a check mark by the answer if I am sure it is correct while I am working.
- Practice basic facts on Internet sites and keep a log of this.
- Keep a log of distributed practice I do (10 minutes per day over 6 days is better than massed practice of 60 minutes in 1 day).
- Line up my work with a ruler to avoid misaligning numbers or get graph paper.
- Re-solve problems with an alternate strategy.

My errors are often **procedural,** so I will:

- Create a check list of steps and check off each as I do them.
- Create a trick for memorizing all the steps
- Do a few minutes of distributed extra practice of all the steps in a procedure every day.

My errors are **conceptual,** so I will:

- Ask for help and set up a time to get it.
- Design diagrams to help me represent my thinking.
- Read explanations from at least two to three Internet sites.
- Create a graphic organizer.

What evidence will you provide that proves you took these steps?

Following every three to four assessments, after students analyze their strengths along with the error types made on each, they submit a pattern analysis to Ms. Musambee, with a list of steps they have taken to overcome these kinds of errors and suggestions for how they can use their identified strengths. As she teaches 100 or more students, she cannot realistically read lengthy reflections by each student or read them after every assessment, and so that is why she has students condense them. Students must also provide evidence to justify their self-reflection conclusions such as examples of strengths or simple errors they have made as well as evidence that they used a strategy, such as an extended distributed practice homework log (see Figure 2.4). One student appeared to have a serious learning challenge because she claimed to spend hours studying for tests, then failed them. When she kept this log, it turned out she didn't study at all. Not all students need to keep such a log, just those with difficulties.

Student Self-Direction **4**

Figure 2.4

Daily Homework Log			
Date	**Time spent working**	**What did I do?** Be very specific—not general "I studied"	**Adult signature— required daily**
Sample: 3/15/11	1.5 hrs	I did extra practice on pg 14 (#s 12–24) and corrected them	

Another option Ms. Musambee offers is having students complete more in-depth, mistake-analysis sheets such as Figure 2.5, in which students select a lengthier problem, analyze what went wrong, and plan steps they will take to avoid making the error again.

Figure 2.5

In-Depth Analysis of Mistakes

Copy incorrect solution here:

Identify what was right as well as where you went wrong in your solution.

_____

_____

_____

_____

What is the correct solution?

_____

_____

_____

_____

State your plan for ensuring that you don't make this mistake again.

_____

_____

_____

_____

The preassessments were then taken out (by those who had chosen to keep theirs) or returned to the majority who had turned theirs in. This happened at the end of the unit after they'd retaken the same format quiz (same concepts but slightly altered numbers) over again. At that point, when the students had to reassess how well they felt that they knew each of the procedures in the opening of the quiz, almost the entire class gave themselves the highest rating. When they corrected this posttest, they all beamed at their gains. One student who had really struggled throughout the unit was thrilled with his 40% increase from the pretest to the posttest. The buzz in the classroom is almost tangible at this point. After receiving differentiated instruction, students celebrate their individual achievement rather than compare final outcome to peers, in which some inevitably do well in comparison and others do not. Furthermore, whether they had chosen option 1, 2 or 3, they all made improvements and fully mastered standard algorithms; Ms. Musambee pointed out that they all "chose well" because they chose what they needed to master the material.

Flexible Student Groups **5**

WHAT IS FORMATIVE ASSESSMENT?

Formative assessments are used to inform next steps needed for all students to succeed, in contrast to summative assessments that summarize learning and are used to compare students' achievement to one another for the purpose of assigning grades. Diagnostic preassessments, like Ms. Musambee's, could be viewed as formative assessment. Yet, formative assessments usually take place during a unit to ascertain what is being learned and to inform whether review is needed or how to take next steps.

At the most basic level, formative assessment means simply using an assessment to inform instructional adjustments. As noted in the Introduction, a powerful large-scale research base backs the significant effectiveness of formative assessment in raising student achievement (Black & Wiliam, 1998). These researchers reviewed 250 research articles and book chapters on formative assessment and found powerful results across many disciplines, including math. As a result, districts nationwide are adopting formative assessment (Dorn, 2010) since it is research-based and therefore meets the requirement of legislation such as No Child Left Behind and Response to Intervention. Particularly in the area of mathematics, in which there is little large-scale research on methods that work, districts are using formative assessment to meet these criteria. In my experience, the teachers who use formative assessment began with small steps and quickly saw exciting gains, further confirming the research findings.

Researchers and theorists have expanded formative assessment to include various closely linked practices. In a nutshell, formative assessment can be contrasted to summative assessment in the analogy of how a physical exam would be contrasted to an autopsy. Essentially, formative assessment provides the information to inform future instructional decisions, much like how information gained from a physical exam might inform health choices we make (Reeves, 2000). According to the research of Black and Wiliam (1998), for assessment to qualify as formative, it must do the following:

- Involve students in self-assessment.
- Convey criteria or learning targets.
- Provide detailed, clear, and specific feedback.
- Engage students in goal-directed behavior.
- Use data to inform next steps and teaching adjustments.
- Recognize the enormous impact of assessment on student confidence and motivation.

More concisely, each of these elements of formative assessment can guide students and teachers in a collaborative effort to answer the following questions, which are commonly used as a uniting framework in formative assessment literature. These could be posted in a classroom and

questions added over the year.

- Where am I?
  - o What do I already know?

- Where am I going?
  - o What are the unit targets I need to learn?

- How will I get there?
  - o What steps will I take to learn the targets?
  - o How will I evaluate my learning along the way?
  - o How can I adjust the steps I'm taking if I'm not mastering the targets or need more challenge?

The preassessment on fractions in Figure 2.1 provided information on which elements of adding and subtracting fractions students knew. Preassessments can also look for more nuanced aspects of understandings and learning inclinations. Rather than just providing discrete feedback on which topics are known and not yet known, preassessments can also reveal where a student is in a learning progression (Heritage, 2008) of conceptual understandings as well as subtle differences in how students think about these concepts, as the preassessment in Figure 2.6 aims to achieve.

Identifying where a student is in a learning progression can make learning a concept less black or white. Instead of either "she gets it" or "she does not get it," formative assessments help both the teacher and students plan for more targeted next steps to take. It is also heartening to see that even if the concept is not fully mastered, data from formative assessments can show that a student still has moved forward toward mastering it. Integers provide an example of a concept that can be difficult to fully master, but steps taken along the way to gain greater proficiency can be noted. These can be broken down and measured. Students who are fully proficient can easily state the rules, apply them accurately, and explain how they work with models. Yet in coming to this proficiency,

Integers Preassessment (with stage indicators bolded)

Core Learning Goals

Do you recall having been exposed to the following learning goals? Circle Y (yes) or N (no).

1. Use and recognize models for representing positive and negative values.	Y	N
2. Represent real-life integer number situations with a model.	Y	N
3. Use symbols to combine positive and negative numbers (*integers*).	Y	N
4. Compare the values of positive and negative numbers.	Y	N
5. Name algorithms for adding and subtracting numbers.	Y	N
6. Explain what opposite numbers are.	Y	N
Learning Extension:		
7. Connect integer symbols to the rules and explain why the rules work.	Y	N

Complete the following:

1. What is the value of the symbols below? ($\oplus$ and $\ominus$ are opposites, so if you match them up what will be the final result? You can express your response in numbers or words.)

$\oplus\oplus\oplus\oplus\oplus\oplus$ $\ominus\ominus\ominus\ominus\ominus$ =

$\ominus\ominus\ominus\ominus\ominus$ $\ominus\ominus\ominus$ =

$\ominus\ominus\ominus\ominus\ominus\ominus\ominus\ominus\ominus$ $\oplus\oplus\oplus\oplus\oplus$ =

$\oplus\oplus\oplus\oplus\oplus\oplus\oplus\oplus\oplus\oplus\oplus$ $\oplus\oplus\oplus$=

2. Suppose the temperature is 10°F. What will the temperature be if it falls (directionally) below zero to –25°F? Draw a picture to support your thinking.

3. Solve.   –255 + 138   –27 – –66

(Continued)

(Continued)

4. Can you draw a model (e.g., chips or number lines) to represent the expressions below? Explain the reasonableness of your model. If you can, use a different model for each.

$-7 + 4$

Model:	Explanation:

$-6 - 8$

Model:	Explanation:

5. Compare using <, >, =.

92 _____ −96   −313 _____ −348   −16 _____ 24

6. Have you learned any rules for adding or subtracting integers? If so, write them below:

7. What is the opposite of 3? Explain how you know.

8. Is the following statement sometimes, always, or never true? Explain your reasoning.

If $x < 0$ and $y > 0$, then $x - y > 0$.

Score your preassessment using the answer key.

Core Learning Goals

Use the data from this preassessment to circle the learning goals you will work on. Circle Y (Yes) or N (No).

I will work on:

1. Use and recognize models for representing positive and negative values.   Y   N

2. Represent real-life integer situations on a model.   Y   N

3. Use symbols to combine positive and negative numbers *(integers)*.   Y   N

4. Compare the values of positive and negative numbers.   Y   N

5. Name algorithms for adding and subtracting numbers.   Y   N

6. Explain what opposite numbers are.   Y   N

Learning Extension:

7. Connect integer symbols to the rules and explain why the rules work.   Y   N

students pass through the following identifiable learning progression, described in Dienes (2000).

In stage one, students are aware that a group with two types of objects has more of some, less of others, or the same amount. Next, in stage two, students can match up the opposing items with one-to-one correspondence and see what (or if any) is left over in a neutralizing model. In stage three, students represent these different items in the more conceptually challenging format of a number line, which is a directional model. Next, in stage four, students use symbols to represent these items in the form of equations, and in the final stages they formalize all of the rules.

Similarly, students encounter predictable patterns of errors when learning about integers, which can be broken down into the four large categories identified in the formative assessment check-in (see Figure 2.7) that follows the preassessment (refer to Figure 2.6). Finding learning progressions and categories of predictable misconceptions need not consume much time. I found various resources that helped me construct this preassessment in a 5-minute search on the Internet (i.e., Dienes, 2000).

Data-Informed Instruction **6**

The integers formative assessment in Figure 2.6 has questions arranged in order of the learning stages so that teachers can identify which stage a student is in. This way, even if at the end of the unit students do not fully grasp all the concepts behind the procedures, they can still identify progress. Also, this formative assessment is designed to uncover whether a student naturally thinks about integers in a directional number line model (moving forward or backward) or an opposite-colored "chip" matching model, with opposites neutralizing each other. Teachers can then teach integers by building on the way in which groups of children are naturally already inclined to think about integers to solidify understanding, then branch out and teach the alternative model. Essentially, the information from the preassessment goes beyond the merely diagnostic level of revealing what students know and don't know. Instead, it seeks to uncover a theory about how a student thinks that can be used to inform more than what, but also how, the material will be taught.

Figure 2.7

Integers Check-In

Solve the problems below:

43 – 8	4 + –15	–9 + 17
–94 – 27	37 + –54	0 – 6

Integers Check-In Self-Assessment

Under "I should have," write in one of the following options:

1. Subtracted when signs differ and kept sign of larger number

2. Always combined same signs and kept their sign

3. Other—explain

Check	Correct	Mistake	I should have:
43 – 81 = –38		124, –124 Combined different signs 38 Didn't keep sign of larger number	
4 + –15 = –11		19, –19 Combined different signs 11 Didn't keep sign of larger number	
–9 + 17 = 8		26, –26 Combined different signs –8 Didn't keep sign of larger number	
–94 – 27 = –121		67, –67 Subtracted same signs 121 Didn't keep same sign	
37 + –37 = 0		74, –74 Combined different signs	
0 – 6 = –6		6 Didn't keep negative sign 4 Tried to borrow	

This preassessment also focuses on using open-ended questions designed to get at students' conceptual thinking, rather than just procedural steps they take. Research has found that math teachers are far more likely to use data to examine procedural errors rather than to explore conceptual misunderstandings, yet spending time investigating conceptual misunderstandings has far more value and impact ultimately on student achievement (Nabors-Oláh, Lawrence, & Riggan, 2010). Furthermore, this research also found that when math teachers used data from formative assessments, the focus on procedural errors rather than conceptual misunderstandings resulted in teachers only addressing procedural errors, and in an almost haphazard way. When they saw errors, they used different teaching strategies to reteach the material, yet these strategies were not directly related to the possible misunderstandings underlying the error patterns. Designing a formative assessment to uncover conceptual misunderstandings may help avoid this shortcoming.

At the same time that this formative assessment was created, a unit plan based on the school's prescribed curriculum and enrichment options was also created (see Figure 2.8). These should always be done together so that the formative assessment or preassessment data are certain to lead right into informing instructional decision-making. This cannot be emphasized enough. So often, well-intended teachers give preassessments but then do not use the information gained to differentiate instruction according to the data gained. This omission is probably the greatest obstacle to using formative assessments to differentiate instruction. Designing the formative assessment and the subsequent unit plan together at the same time overcome this problem. Though the following may appear to be overly prescriptive, it is meant instead to serve as a guideline of how a teacher might think about planning. Of course, teacher expertise is needed to make exceptions or fine-tune such a plan, as needed for the individual students being taught.

Note that the unit plan numbering in Figure 2.8 is matched to the numbering of the Core Learning Goals on the formative assessment in Figure 2.6. (Note also in Figure 2.6 that the numbering of the list of unit targets is matched to the numbering of the questions that follow.)

WHERE AM I?

INVOLVING STUDENTS IN SELF-ASSESSMENT

Preassessment Options

Diagnostic preassessments are given before units begin to help students answer the question "Where am I?" The results are then used by teachers and students to determine next steps to take. This information can be obtained through structured diagnostic preassessments like the one designed by Ms. Musambee or through other premade preassessments

Figure 2.8

Sample Unit Plan Options

Determined With Formative Assessment Data Results

1. Use and recognize models for representing positive and negative values.

   If unknown—do intro and lesson 1
   If partially known—do only lesson 1

2. Use models to represent positive and negative numbers *(integers)*.

   If unknown—lesson 2

3. Combine the values of positive and negative numbers.

   If unknown—lesson 3

4. Represent real-life integer number situations on a number line model.

   If unknown—lesson 4

   Those who seem inclined to learn from chips—do lesson 5 on chips

   Those who seem inclined to learn from number line—do lesson 6 on number line

   When comfortable—do both models

5. Compare positive and negative number expressions or equations without a model.

   If unknown—lesson 7

6. Name algorithms for adding and subtracting numbers.

   If unknown—lesson 8

7. Explain what opposite numbers are.

   If unknown—p. 5 Intro

Practice Algorithm and Check-In

- Find classic errors. (Identify what kind)

- Use practice to address those errors and manipulatives, if needed.

Learning Extension:

8. If students do not know the absolute value questions, they can do that parallel curricular unit. If they do know this, go to full set of learning challenges.

Sources for Additional Materials to Have Ready for the Unit—If Needed

General

http://nrich.maths.org/5961 An article about the history of negative numbers. NRICH

http://www.mathleague.com/help/integers/integers.htm A reference page for integers, absolute value, and addition and subtraction algorithms. MathLeague

Reinforcement/Practice

http://nrich.maths.org/5947 An activity that would reinforce/supplement for students who are having trouble using the chip model to represent integers and integer problems. NRICH http://nrich.maths.org/5911 An online game to help students practice adding and subtracting with positive and negative numbers. (A small range of numbers: –6 through 6.) NRICH

http://www.mathgoodies.com/lessons/vol5/challenge_vol5.html Word problems for extra practice that reflect real-life situations. Math Goodies

http://www.ehow.com/how_5066953_teach-negative-numbers-card-game.html A card game to practice adding integers. eHow

http://www.funbrain.com/guess2/index.html A FunBrain game giving a range of practice with all integer operations. FunBrain

http://www.dositey.com/2008/index.php?page=free_activities&sub=58&subsub=m A website with skill-related games and practice for adding and subtracting integers. Dositey

http://nlvm.usu.edu/en/nav/frames_asid_161_g_2_t_1.html This virtual manipulative models adding integers with chips. Library of Virtual Manipulatives

http://nlvm.usu.edu/en/nav/frames_asid_162_g_2_t_1.html This virtual manipulative models subtracting integers with chips. Library of Virtual Manipulatives

Challenge

http://nrich.maths.org/5872 A challenge activity to conjecture how negative numbers impact algebraic expressions. NRICH

http://nrich.maths.org/5868 A challenge activity to conjecture what happens when adding/subtracting consecutive integers. NRICH

http://nrich.maths.org/481 A challenge activity to discover 5 missing addends. When paired, they produce different sums. NRICH

http://www.figurethis.org/challenges/c46/challenge.htm Time zones as an application of integers. FigureThis!

http://mathforum.org/library/drmath/view/61125.html When was King George born? A problem that requires thinking along a number line to find relative ages. Dr. Math

Compiled by Julie Fila, Wellesley Public Schools Middle School Math Teacher.

available from a variety of sources. Information can also be obtained less formally by having students self-correct class work or homework. Often teachers feel that they know where students are, so they omit the preassessment. Teachers are sometimes surprised by what is found when they do give a preassessment. During a recent debate on whether to give a preassessment, one teacher who doubted its value was reminded by another teacher that the preassessment is also for the students so that they can self-score it and get a realistic sense of what they do and don't know.

Alternative (to the examples given in this chapter) comprehensive preassessments can be designed even more simply, as the sample preassessment on polynomials in Figure 2.9 shows, or taken from a source such as a unit test in a textbook. Textbooks such as those published by Glencoe (Day et al., 2009) have well-designed preassessments that serve to assess not only the unit objectives, but the prerequisite skills needed for the unit as well. Although current versions of certain math programs such as the Connected Mathematics Program (CMP) (Lappan, Fey, Fitzgerald, Friel, & Phillips, 2006) do not include preassessments or posttests, older versions of this program have, and so these can be used. CMP also includes a helpful test-question generator. Also, tests that can be used as preassessments can sometimes be found on the Internet.

Figure 2.9

Sample Polynomials Preassessment

1. Write with exponents: $7 \cdot 7 \cdot 7 \cdot 7$

2. Write with exponents: $y \cdot y \cdot y \cdot y$

3. Simplify: $2a + 4a$

4. Simplify: $3m + 2n - m + 4w$

5. Write using exponents: $x \cdot x \cdot y \cdot y \cdot y \cdot y$

6. Simplify: $5(2x + 3y)$

7. Simplify: $x(3x - 4)$

8. Arrange the terms of $4x^2 - 2x^4 - 3 + 2x$ so that the powers of x are in descending order.

9. Simplify: $(4x + 8) + (7x + y - 6)$

10. Simplify: $(4x + 3y - 2) - (2x - 2y + 1)$

11. Expand: $-2n(3n^2 + 2n)$

12. Expand and simplify: $2a(2a + 7) + 7(2a + 7)$

My corrections show that I can:

1. Use exponents

2. Use exponents with variables

3. Combine like terms

4. Combine like terms/unlike terms

5. Use exponents with multiple variables

6. Distribute a number

7. Distribute a variable

8. Order powers

9. Add trinomials

10. Subtract trinomials

11. Can distribute term with coefficient

12. Can do multiple step expansion and simplification

Teachers can also simply ask students to write all they know about a topic for 10 minutes before beginning the unit. When we did this before beginning a unit on percentages, we received the following continuum of responses shown below:

- Developing Knowledge
  - A percent is when you use the symbol %.
  - Percent has to do with sales.

- Adequate Knowledge
  - o Percent is part of 100.
  - o It is like a fraction.

- Advanced Knowledge
  - o Percents are used to convert numbers to equivalent ratios, with 100 serving as the common base in order to make quick and easy comparisons among them.

Teachers can use K-W-L (know, want to learn, learned) charts before units, asking students to write what they already know about a topic such as percentage, and what they want to learn. Students can later revisit these and add what they learned. For an instant preassessment, teachers can ask for a show of hands to see what percentage of the class already knows certain points, and then adjust the lesson accordingly. This is a great way to activate prior knowledge and help students connect new information to what they already know about the topic.

Teachers can also give preassessments as homework and clearly mark on them that students should not receive assistance with them. If an honor code is established and students understand that the purpose of the assessment is not to evaluate them but to understand them and to use the information to differentiate instruction and best meet their needs, then students are less inclined to use supports that might skew the assessment.

Summary of Preassessment Options

- Self-created tests
- Test in textbooks such as published by Glencoe
- Internet
- Open-ended questions
- Homework

Tips for Preassessing

When introducing preassessments to students, emphasize that this is a chance to show what they have been taught so that the teacher does not reteach what they already know. Stating it this way externalizes the assessment so that it is an assessment of what they have learned rather than of how smart they are. Students can feel unnerved when they see a preassessment that has information that they do not know. Prerequisites should be included in preassessments, but still there will be some questions they have never seen before. Over time, they will begin to see the tremendous value and usefulness of preassessments. Yet initially, they need to be introduced very sensitively. Some teachers tell students, "Sometimes even the students who are typically the strongest get a zero on a preassessment. This means nothing—just that they haven't seen the material before. What matters is knowing what you know and what you don't know, and the preassessment helps you do this. Once you know this, you can better focus your studying, then use your time more efficiently." If they still need to be put even more at ease, the preassessment can open by asking them to tell what they do know about the topic in a KEWLW (what I know and an example, what I want to learn, what I have learned and an example) format so that they can acknowledge and feel good about what they already know.

Also, preassessments should be as brief as possible so that they don't take up much in class time because students often don't know material on them, unless you are preassessing the prerequisites for new material for a new unit. In addition, preassessments can be constructed so that they offer a valuable learning experience as well so that teaching time is not lost. Teachers I know who most vigilantly guard their time find that at a minimum they can do one preassessment per unit, and these should not take up a full class period. Doing only one full unit preassessment and perhaps one briefer formal formative assessment check-in (again this need not fill up the entire class period either) is more than enough to see noteworthy student achievement in our experience and according to the research (Tieso, 2005), as long as the information gained is systematically used to inform instruction.

When students do not know something on a preassessment, they can be encouraged to write HLY ("haven't learned yet") rather than DK ("don't know"), again because this suggests that you are looking at what they have been taught rather than how intelligent they are. Furthermore, briefer preassessments might be less stressful for students. To further minimize the stress, students can be told that they will self-correct the preassessments so that they do not worry about what the teacher will think. They can also be reassured that they will get to retake it (not with the exact same numbers, but with a similar format and same concepts). This can both motivate them to self-direct their learning during the unit and to maximize how much they learn, as well as make it less stressful. This claim is based on experiences that I have had in my own teaching and have seen in other classrooms; after students take a preassessment, some continuously refer back to the essential unit learnings that the preassessments showed they needed to address. Some then want to gain greater proficiency with these and put in extra effort to do so.

Whether formal preassessments or less formal methods are used to gather data on where students are, it is important to have students correct their own work, as research has found that this practice dramatically uplifts achievement, while scoring peers' work or having work scored for one is less effective (Heritage & Niemi, 2006). Preassessments can also be designed to activate background knowledge so that instead of being viewed as lost instructional time, they can promote learning. For example, asking a student to solve $1/2 + 1/4$ and then asking students to draw a diagram or imagine a pizza might actually lead them to rethink their computation if they had made the error of applying whole number strategies to this problem (and so got 2/6). Thus they are learning during the preassessment.

Preassessments should include final challenge questions so that teachers can test outwards until they do find some areas that even high-achieving students can benefit from learning. Conversely, preassessments should also cover prerequisite skills so that those students who do not know the material can be tested backward to the point where they do know material. With this information, teachers can pinpoint which backfilling they might need to do before beginning a unit. In addition, teachers I have worked with have designed some preassessments and found, surprisingly, that students can only do 10% when they had predicted that students knew much more.

Summary of Tips for Preassessments

- Introduce preassessments carefully.
- Keep them brief.
- Coach students to write HLY for "haven't learned yet" rather than DK for "don't know."
- Design preassessments to activate learning.
- Have students self-score them.
- Include challenges and cover prerequisites.

Continuous Formative Assessment

3 After taking the first and most basic step of diagnostic preassessment, then using the results to plan instruction and help students know where they are and the next steps needed, teachers can continue to use formative assessment concurrently with instruction throughout the unit. Teachers already regularly score homework and class work and so get a sense of where students are. Formative assessment asks that this be done more systematically and extend out to include urging students to self-assess their own work more systematically. Because teachers often just don't have time to analyze all student work, emphasizing students' self-scoring is also just practical. Furthermore, adolescents often believe they have mastered concepts, when their grasp may still be shaky. Continuous formative assessments give them a stronger, more realistic sense of where they are more frequently.

4 Students can be guided to regularly self-assess their class work, assessments, and homework for accuracy through using self-checking, error-detection methods, such as doing the inverse of operations, plugging the solution back into problems and then checking their work, or re-solving the problem to make sure that they get the same answer the second time, and if they don't, then self-assessing what they did wrong. They can also self-assess their work's accuracy with answer keys. While taking tests or

doing any problems, they can be taught to check off each problem that they are certain is correct. Essentially, students should develop the habit of self-assessing work themselves with error-detection strategies as well as with answer keys and rubrics so frequently that they become linked in students' minds. Work should not feel complete to students until they have checked it. Self-scoring enables students to receive timely, specific, understandable feedback that focuses on next steps, which are three qualities of effective feedback, according to Wiggins (1998). As students continuously self-assess their work, they can be coached to identify patterns in their errors and to find underlying issues that block them from achieving as well as they can. For example, students analyzed their mistakes on Ms. Musambee's preassessments within the framework of simple factual, procedural, or computation errors. Often, teachers seek reasons for students' errors, yet having students take the lead in this process allows them to experience beneficial deep processing. They derive valuable feedback that would not be possible from a teacher with a typical load of close to or above 100 students.

Students can complete an analysis with a format like that shown in Figure 2.3, then collate the findings from three of these and turn in a self-reflection with evidence of steps taken to address self-identified underlying error patterns. In addition to scoring preassessments, homework, and class work, students can engage in periodic structured self-assessment check-ins, like that shown in Figure 2.10. Moreover, after taking quizzes

---

Figure 2.10

Equations Check-In

Copy the solution (though there are multiple ways to arrive at this solution) from the board:

$Y + Y + 16 = 4Y + 10 - 2$

Steps I used to solve this:

☐ All basic calculations were correct.
☐ Combined like terms.
☐ Subtracted term with smaller coefficients from both sides.
☐ Subtracted smaller constants from both sides.
☐ Divided both sides by the coefficient of the variable.

and tests, students can also reflect on the effort they put into preparing for tests and steps they took.

In addition to scoring their work for accuracy and looking for error patterns, students can also be helped to determine potential conceptual misunderstandings. For example, with fractions, a teacher was alerted to recognize the most common misunderstandings about fractions because her research indicated that students often do the following:

- See fractions as two separate whole numbers and therefore apply whole number strategies and logic.
- Have insufficient exposure to fractions, causing them to have difficulty imagining if their answer makes sense.
- Misapply rote recipes they have learned, but not understood, in the past (Newstead & Murray, 1998).

Students can use data from their self-scored preassessments to check off which of these misunderstandings they may have had. Teacher knowledge of such common misunderstandings and why they occur is critical to formative assessment, as is student self-knowledge.

Furthermore, students can engage in simple ongoing formative assessment by regularly writing reflections at the end of the class on how well they understood the topic, or on their homework, projects, or anything that they turn in. The format shown in Figure 2.11 can be posted to remind students to jot down their reflections regularly. Students can also indicate responses by standing/sitting, using whiteboards, lifting a red/green stick

Figure 2.11

Reflection Guide

How is my understanding of the current topic?

❒ Need more learning
❒ Seems okay
❒ I'm ready for a challenge
❒ Other _____

Based on today's work, a question I have is:

_____

_____

_____

_____

or cup they have on their desk, or using technology mechanisms such as pressing a button that lights up on a teacher computerboard (if available).

Progress Monitoring

Another more structured and research-based format for continuous formative assessment is the aspect of curriculum-based measurement (CBM) that involves progress monitoring. A robust research base has shown progress monitoring uplifts achievement, particularly when teachers use systematic data-based decision-making rules and skills analysis feedback gained from the progress measures' data to inform program modifications (Stecker, Fuchs, & Fuchs, 2005). In addition, The What Works Clearing House Mathematics K–8 Practice Guide also recommends progress monitoring as a research-based practice found to enhance learning (Gersten et al., 2009).

In this model, brief (8–10 minutes) and easy-to-administer probes are given weekly or every 2 weeks. These probes are similar to the check-ins in Figures 2.7 and 2.10, The scores from these probes are then graphed. These probes can assess core competencies (computation, applications, concepts—see http://AIMSweb.com or http://easycbm.com for examples) that correlate highly to scores on annual state tests. (We found strong correlations [0.65 and higher] when we correlated our students' AIMSweb computation probe scores to their scores on our state assessments.) When students show gains on these weekly probe scores, those gains would also indicate that the scores that they would receive on annual standardized state tests would also be increasing. These probes cover content from the general grade-level curriculum across all schools.

Alternatively, these types of probes can more closely resemble the curriculum used when they are designed using *curricular sampling*, items sampled from one's full annual curriculum to assess mastery of the actual curriculum being taught. Curricular sampling measures are drawn from the annual objectives of the specific curriculum taught and so are often more appealing for progress measuring because they additionally offer diagnostic information that immediately helps teachers tailor their instruction within their specific curriculum. However, the usefulness of these measures in lifting achievement is not yet as established as it is for the reading measures and elementary mathematics measures. A theoretical and research overview of progress monitoring, as well as a practitioner's description of her experiences with using progress-monitoring probes in an algebra class, is provided in Foegen and Morrison (2010).

Recent work on algebra assessment and instruction by Foegen, Olson, and Impecoven-Lind (2008) and on Accelerated Math (Ysseldyke & Tardrew, 2007) looks promising and provides many practical probes that could be used to measure progress as well as for diagnostic purposes, if they match one's school's curriculum closely enough. Teachers can adapt this model by creating probes that they design themselves, based on their own curriculum, to measure progress toward achieving a smaller goal such as unit objectives. The most recent research has found that the shorter the cycle between gathering data in a formative assessment model and using that data to inform instruction and provide feedback, the better in terms of students' achievement gains (Bulkley, Nabors Oláh, & Blanc, 2010). Therefore, the probes or check-ins should ideally be done and scored within one class period.

If standard probes are used, such as those available at AIMSweb or http://easycbm.com, after they are scored, students can find errors patterns made in them so that they can receive additional diagnostic feedback as well. AIMSweb is a pay site, yet we preferred those probes because they had 40 problems, so were more useful diagnostically. http://easycbm .com/ is a free site, but the probes are far briefer and are multiple choice.

The question of "Where am I?" can be answered initially with self-scoring global diagnostic preassessments as well as all throughout a unit as students continuously self-score class work and homework with methods as simple as putting a check by answers they have found correct using answer keys, or the more structured progress-monitoring models of continuous formative assessment, just described. All in all, students should habitually pause and discover where they stand in mastering each element of a new unit, ideally regularly noting this in a backward-design model (Wiggins & McTighe, 2005), in which they constantly assess their progress toward mastering a list of clearly stated unit targets.

WHERE AM I GOING?

CONVEYING CRITERIA OR LEARNING TARGETS

Students can determine where they are going when they clearly understand the unit's targets. Teachers who use a backward design model (Wiggins & McTighe, 2005), in which they clarify for themselves each end-of-unit criteria before beginning a new unit, are in the best position to convey these to students. Of course, with procedural computation targets, the criteria of achieving these are straightforward in that the procedures should be accurately performed. These can be merely listed as Core Learning Goals on a preassessment, as Figure 2.6 shows. However, the National Council of Teachers of Mathematics standards (NCTM, 2000) have encouraged teachers to place greater emphasis on developing student thinking along lines such as explaining and justifying responses, and the criteria for exemplary justifications can be less straightforward. This can be done through rubrics, practice scoring justifications, and detailed feedback.

Conveyed Unit Targets **2**

Conveying targets for conceptual proficiency is also challenging—specific and detailed rubrics that show continua of understandings offer one way to do this, as shown in Figure 2.10.

Criteria for Scoring Justifications

The NCTM recommends that students frequently practice justifying the reasonabless of their responses. This can be a powerful opportunity for students to clarify and defend their thinking. In the first part of Figure 2.12, students are asked to find the mean, median, and mode, answer a question, and justify their answer. Some students will require supports in learning to write a strong justification, and they could analyze exemplary justifications like those in Figure 2.12 with a rubric (Figure 2.13). In the two example justifications, scoring with a rubric reveals that the second justification is weaker because the student does not directly address the outlier score as the key point or inference, though the writer does hint at it. Next, students could write and score practice justifications for homework and self-score them with rubrics. Teachers would need to read and score these as well, perhaps with a different color pen on the same rubric. The students would use feedback to rewrite, then rescore their justifications, highlighting or underlining the improvements and attaching the revision to the prior attempt.

Though this process is time consuming for teachers, the importance of the skill of writing exemplary justifications merits the time investment. Through this kind of model analysis, application, and self-evaluative practice, students identify and understand the criteria for strong justifications and therefore understand the targets they are aiming for, which is critical to formative assessment.

Criteria for Concept Mastery

Conveying criteria for how to determine whether students have mastered concepts presents more complex challenges. For example, what are the targets for showing one understands the concept behind dividing fractions? Students may perform the algorithm rotely but not understand the concept. Perhaps having students explain with diagrams why it works or apply it across varied and real-life word problem situations might be targets they should aim for. Students should also be given opportunities in some units, perhaps having been given model lists of targets, to learn the process of uncovering these for themselves. This prepares them for future classrooms and life situations in which targets may not be explicitly conveyed but are still critical to uncover. Students can be coached to attend to cues in the hidden curriculum—those regular practices in schools with an unnoticed and almost invisible quality, such as that a new unit directly follows most unit tests or assessments. Students could generate lists of ways they could discover the new targets, such as previewing the new unit's contents or looking over the end-of unit review. Students should then list the targets and do a preassessment themselves by attempting a unit review. This processing provides a deeper familiarity with the targets and alerts them to the specific content they need to learn.

Figure 2.12

Sample Justifications

Tom scored 22, 77, 81, 74, 83, 85, 91, and 74 on his math quizzes. Find the mean, median, and mode. Which would be the best to use to determine the final grade and why?

1. I believe the score should be the median (79) because he only bombed one test. This should not be held against him. The average (73.4) makes the score too low because of this, especially since the trend is increasing, the one low score might mean he was sick or did not understand the quiz format.

2. I believe his score should be the average (73.4). These are the scores he received, and the average is usually used to give a grade, not the median (79). His scores were going up, which shows an upward trend, but this is not a factor when calculating grades, though it could be considered if he is between two close grades.

Figure 2.13

Justification Rubric

Score: (Categories listed below)	4 Outstanding	3 Proficient	2 Nearing Proficient	1 Not Yet Proficient
Complete and Accurate Math	Fully Complete and Accurate	Math is Complete and Accurate, but for a Small Simple Error That Is Reasonable	Math Is Complete and Accurate, but for a Few Small Simple Errors That Are Reasonable	Math Is Incomplete and Inaccurate
Key Point or Inference Identified	Overtly States the Key Point or Clearly Identifies the Inference	A Piece of Evidence Is Provided	Hints at Evidence	No Evidence
Clear Opinion	Clear Opinion Stated	Opinion Is Clear, but Not Fully Stated	Opinion Unclear	Opinion Not Stated
Solid Evidence to Support Opinion	Exceptionally Strong or Multiple Pieces of Supportive Evidence Are Given to Back Up Opinion	A Piece of Evidence Is Stated	Hints at Evidence	No Evidence
Evaluates Reasonableness of Opinion	Gives a Compelling, Direct Statement of Why the Opinion Is Reasonable	Suggests Why Opinion Is Reasonable	Reasonableness Is Unclear	Opinion Seems to Have No Reasonable Basis

HOW WILL I GET THERE?

PROVIDING FEEDBACK

Achieving learning goals requires the recursive process of using continuous formative feedback to inform and readjust the next steps. Students derive feedback from self-assessment constantly, as they use strategies to check their work while doing it and through using answer keys. Teachers provide feedback when they review tests, quizzes, projects, class activities, discussions, or other student work.

Detailed, Clear, and Specific Feedback

Feedback that advises the next steps to be taken has been found to be far more effective than feedback that evaluates (Hattie & Timperley, 2007), yet this needs to be done in a time-efficient way. Generating time-efficient ways such as using the structured format presented earlier (Figure 2.7) or limiting the number of feedback statements given is critical. Research has found that providing clear specific advice results in far greater future achievement than does summative feedback such as grades or number correct (Elawar & Corno, 1985). The least valuable is feedback about the person such as "Great student!" (Hattie & Timperely, 2007).

In a landmark study on the effects of feedback given on mathematics homework, Elawar and Corno (1985) found that writing comments rather than giving a score of number correct on homework uplifted student achievement. The teachers in this study used instructions and praise. This kind of feedback conveys a sense of hope that students can and will improve. As a result of such supportive feedback, they are more likely to sink their teeth into their work. For example, one student never appreciated vacuous praise, yet devoured suggestions for how she could specifically improve and then took tremendous pride in her improvement. This example underscores the importance of students being given opportunities to use the feedback that they receive on assignments that will give them the satisfaction of seeing improvements. Specifically, when students completed the adding and subtracting fractions preassessment, they worked on this topic for several weeks and were given tremendous amounts of formative feedback. When they repeated taking this assessment (with similar content from the first preassessment in a similarly formatted assessment) at the end of the unit and compared their scores with the preassessment, they obtained satisfaction from seeing their progress.

Teachers can provide feedback in various ways. Teachers can convey feedback instantly through task checklists (refer to Figure 2.6) or rubrics (refer to Figure 2.13). Furthermore, teachers can write on assignments recommendations to use specific alternative strategies or explain ways to work more effectively, as Ms. Musambee provided to Shanti.

$$27.6 \times 104.07$$

$$\begin{array}{r} 104.07 \\ \times \ 27.60 \\ \hline 00000 \\ 624420 \\ 7284900 \\ 20814000 \\ \hline 2\,872.332 \end{array}$$

Shanti,

You remembered rules for multiplying decimals. Next time, you don't need to line up the decimals. This caused you to add an unnecessary zero, which was inefficient and slowed you down.

Good luck on the test! Looks like you are well ready.—Ms. Musambee

Feedback like this is time consuming, and so teachers might just write one such note on each child's work, and not do so regularly. Given how time demanding this kind of feedback is for teachers, students should write a note back ensuring that they understand the feedback and explaining when they will use it. Teachers I have worked with have shared that they have written comments that students do not appear to have read. The note could be included in the weekly homework packets they turn in and could include evidence that shows where/how they used the feedback.

Feedback on Processes Students Use

When teachers provide feedback, in addition to ensuring that it is timely, specific, detailed, and understandable to the learner, they should also focus on providing equal or more feedback on processes students use rather than just on task accuracy, as research has found this is more powerful (Hattie & Timperley, 2007). For instance, if a student set up an equation all over a page of scrap paper, providing feedback that recommends using graph paper or folding the paper to create straighter lines can be more useful than just noting where the student began miscalculation as the numbers became misaligned.

Also, providing feedback and advice on how students internally self-regulate their thinking while working yields greater gains than accuracy feedback (Hattie & Timperley, 2007). Teachers can note that a student used excellent error-detection strategies by checking the solution in the margin, but then did not use appropriate fix-up strategies to correct an error such as realigning the numbers or drawing an alternative diagram.

A formative assessment tool for exploring what processes students use when solving word problems is the Mathematical Processing Instrument (Hegarty & Kozhevnikov, 1999; see Figure 2.14). This instrument allows

Figure 2.14

Mathematical Processing Instrument

1. At each of the two ends of a straight path, a man planted a tree and then every 5 m along the path he planted another tree. The length of the path is 15 m. How many trees were planted?

2. On one side of a scale there is a 1 kg weight and half a brick. On the other side there is one full brick. The scale is balanced. What is the weight of the brick?

3. A balloon first rose 200 m from the ground, then moved 100 m to the east, then dropped 100 m. It then traveled 50 m to the east, and finally dropped straight to the ground. How far was the balloon from its original starting point?

4. In an athletics race, Jim is 4 m ahead of Tom and Peter is 3 m behind Jim. How far is Peter ahead of Tom?

5. A square (A) has an area of 1 m². Another square (B) has sides twice as long. What is the area of B?

6. From a long stick of wood, a man cut 6 short sticks, each 2 feet long. He then found he had a piece of 1 foot long left over. Find the length of the original stick.

7. The area of a rectangular field is 60 m². If its length is 10 meters, how far would you have traveled if you walked the whole way around the field?

8. Jack, Paul, and Brian all have birthdays on the 1st of January, but Jack is 1 year older than Paul and Jack is 3 years younger than Brian. If Brian is 10 years old, how old is Paul?

9. The diameter of a tin of peaches is 10 cm. How many tins will fit in a box 30 cm by 40 cm (one layer only)?

10. Four young trees were set out in a row 10 m apart. A well was situated beside the last tree. A bucket of water is needed to water two trees. How far would a gardener have to walk altogether if he had to water the four trees using only one bucket?

11. A hitchhiker set out on a journey of 60 miles. He walked the first 5 miles and then got a lift from a lorry driver. When the driver dropped him off, he still had half of his journey to travel. How far had he traveled in the lorry?

12. How many picture frames 6 cm long and 4 cm wide can be made from a piece of framing 200 cm long?

13. On one side of a scale there are three pots of jam and a 100 g weight. On the other side there are a 200 g and a 500 g weight. The scale is balanced. What is the weight of a pot of jam?

14. A ship was traveling northwest. It made a turn of 90 degrees to the right. An hour later it made a turn through 45 degrees to the left. In what direction was it then traveling?

15. There are 8 animals on a farm. Some of them are hens and some are rabbits. Between them they have 22 legs. How many hens and how many rabbits are on the farm?

Source: Hegarty & Kozhevnikov, 1999.

Scoring the MPI:

1. The first score was the number of problems solved correctly.

2. Second, whether the student used a visual image while solving each problem was recorded. For each problem where the student did not use a visual image, a score of 0 was given. A score of 1 was given on each problem for which the student used a visual image.

(Continued)

(Continued)

3. The third and fourth scores, based on Hegarty and Kozhevnikov's (1999) study, measured the extent to which the students' visual images were either pictorial or schematic.

a. A visual image was scored as primarily pictorial if the student reported or drew an image of the objects or persons referred to in the problem. For example, consider the responses to the following problems:

Problem 1: The diameter of a can of peaches is 10 units. How many cans will fit in a box 30 units by 40 units (one layer only)?

Problem 2: On one side of a scale, there are three pots of jam and a 100-oz. weight. On the other side, there is a 200-oz. and a 500-oz. weight. The scale is balanced. What is the weight of one pot of jam?

The following imagery reported in Problems 1 and 2, respectively, was scored as primarily pictorial: All I see is like, a little can of peaches and, like, a lot of other cans. A weight balance with pots of jam on each side. A number of diagrams drawn by the students were categorized as being primarily pictorial.

b. A visual image was scored as primarily schematic if the student drew a diagram, used gestures showing the spatial relations between objects in a problem in explaining the solution strategy, or reported a spatial image of the relations expressed in the problem. The following responses for Problems 1 and 2, respectively, were scored as being primarily schematic imagery:

I did 10 into 30 and 10 into 40 and I added, no, multiplied them. [Probe: Did you see a picture of the problem in your mind while you were solving it?] It was a box and it said 30 and 40 on each side and there were cans going across that said 10 and vertical.

There was a scale balanced with a 500 and 200 weight on one side and 100 ounce and 3 pots of jam on the other side.

Source: Van Garderen, 2006.

teachers to determine whether students use diagrams or pictures when solving word problems. Teachers can then use this preassessment to assess the quality and sophistication of the students' diagrams (Van Garderen, 2006). If students have inefficient approaches to creating diagrams, teachers can use guiding strategies, which are explained in Chapter 5.

Feedback to Engage Students in Goal-Directed Behavior

When students receive clear, specific feedback that provides advice for how they can better achieve mastering the unit targets, motivation can be kindled. Following preassessments, students can be coached to quickly set goals of getting 20% more correct. However, extensive goal setting has not been found effective in some studies (Gersten et al., 2009), perhaps because teachers have so little instructional time and using class or homework time to write lengthy goals may detract from time spent actually learning math. Instead, goals should be fostered as a continuous force that is alive all the time as students use feedback to make adjustments to their learning so that they can pursue mastering the current topic.

Student-Driven Feedback

Often students believe it is the responsibility of teachers to take the lead in providing guidance and next steps to take, which is true. However the strongest students do this regularly as well, detecting errors in their work and mentally planning for how to correct them and avoid them in the future. Students could then be coached to write such feedback to themselves after self-scoring work, and teachers could eyeball it to check off if they agree, or revise the feedback as appropriate. It is important that students act habitually on all feedback, and so, as part of their next assignment, they need to demonstrate in a note at the end how they used prior teacher feedback in this assignment, or feedback and next steps that they had generated themselves.

Next Steps and Adjustments

A classic difficulty with formative assessment is teachers giving a preassessment, looking it over, and then teaching the unit with minimal adjustments made. This will not achieve the positive effects on student learning that the formative assessment research base has found. Both teachers and students must actively use the data from preassessments to make instructional adjustments and to determine next steps for learning (Wiliam, 2010), the more data driven and structured the better. Using data to determine grouping is one of the most primary and obvious adjustments teachers can make. Data can also be used to make instructional adjustments. For example, one teacher gave a geometry preassessment and surprisingly discovered how much students already knew, and so he omitted everything that they already knew from his teaching plans. On some items, the class was mixed, and so he planned to do readiness-level groups for teaching those points. For the items that nobody knew, he planned some full-class lesson activities based on student interests.

Another teacher has students use data to decide next steps by giving a practice test a day or so before a real unit test, not in order to teach to the test but to provide experience with test taking such as time management. Then, he has students self-score the practice test and note what steps they need to do to prepare for the actual unit test. He is sure to include several highly challenging questions so that everyone who takes the test will gain something from the experience. Ideally, students can create their own tests—however, these are more difficult to score. A debriefing format for student reflections after taking a practice test could include such starter statements as:

I had difficulty with the following:

I need to remember the following when I take the actual test:

IMPACT OF ASSESSMENT ON CONFIDENCE AND MOTIVATION

Teachers who use preassessments and formative assessment feedback should keep in mind a few cautions. Feedback about the person yields the smallest and possibly a negative impact (Hattie & Timperley, 2007), as the following story illustrates:

> *Anu had struggled with math since day one. By seventh grade, she developed ego-protecting and coping mechanisms that minimized how much her poor grades upset her but unfortunately also resulted in her minimizing her effort. Following a unit with intensive formative assessment, she received one the highest grades ever on her final unit test. Her well-intended teacher pulled her aside, and in an attempt to use the chance to bolster Anu's self-esteem and effort, suggested "Maybe you are actually good at math, as this test clearly shows." Anu beamed and did increase her efforts. However, when she performed less well on the next test because the unit was based on another topic that was more of a struggle for her, she was emotionally devastated. She had opened herself up to care and invest in math, and her coping strategies were therefore weakened when she needed them.*

Instead of offering a personal comment, Anu's teacher could have pointed out the external factors, such as the formative assessment instruction, how that unit's content was not an area she had struggled with as much in the past, and how she had spent more time on her homework. These factors she could understand and control, and that feedback might have been a safer route for motivating her.

Teachers should also recognize that preassessments can initially lead to problems in self-esteem if students are not used to taking them and find that although they usually are in the highest math group, occasionally preassessments scores will suggest that they need some shoring up of foundational skills for certain units. For example, Piers did not perform well on a preassessment on ratio so was put in a group with students who needed similar practice, but he felt the work was to be easy (it wasn't) and so went home and cried because he felt that the work that he was then being given was beneath him. Teachers need to keep such stories in mind and exercise caution, as well as paying close attention to the norms that they set up in their classrooms, to avoid these kinds of reactions.

These stories illustrate difficulties that can arise during formative assessment. Black and Wiliam (1998) also refer to the impact of grades on confidence and motivation. One of our students, Joanna, had struggled with math since day one. Despite being conscientious, she often failed tests and quizzes. By sixth grade, she'd come to expect this but still felt disappointed every time. When she took her first formative assessment preassessment, she was thrilled that it didn't count and excited to know that she would get a chance to retake it after the unit so that she would have a chance to improve her score. She worked diligently all through the unit, requesting extra practice for those problem types she knew she needed yet to master. When she went from a 40% to an 85%, she felt on top of the world. She never asked how she scored in comparison to her peers she just celebrated her own improvement and how much she had learned. Formative assessment shifts the focus away from comparison to peers and toward one's own gains and movement toward mastering clear targets.

This chapter has provided an overview of the central practices in getting started with formative assessment. Formative assessment teaching practices that lead into differentiating instruction include strategies such as using questions to both extract formative assessment and tiering instruction for varied levels within a class. These and other practices are explored in the following chapters on tiering, meeting the needs of students who are low achieving, and meeting the challenges of students who are high achieving.

3

Tiered Instruction

Before class Ms. Chou reviewed the preassessments she had given the day before on parallel lines. She had been surprised to find that some of her eighth-grade students had not been able to define clearly parallel lines, though a few were fully able to and could even find measures of the angles when two parallel lines were cut by a transversal and only one angle measure was given. As always, the preassessment revealed a range of readiness levels and some surprises.

As her students entered, they turned in their homework packets for the week. A few were placed in the bin "I have questions," but most put theirs in the bin labeled "I'm comfortable with my understanding of this topic." Ms. Chou usually sets aside a few minutes at the end of class to review any homework questions with those who placed theirs in the first bin, while other students work on extensions. At this point in the year Ms. Chou has established a class climate where learning differences are all valued. Because students recognize that "we are here to get what we need" to learn, there is almost no stigma, and probably more respect, for kids being forthright about acknowledging their needs. Today Ms. Chou begins class with a quick review of vocabulary terms and asks students to define terms such as parallel lines, transversal, supplemental, complementary, corresponding, alternate interior and vertical angles. A few students who had shown mastery of the concepts and correctly defined these on the preassessment discretely move along more quickly and begin to use these terms to solve some extended challenges posted on the board (see Figure 3.1).

The rest of the class works on the foundational task of learning the vocabulary words and seems not to take note of the other students who have begun the extensions. Ms. Chou then asks the class an open-ended question about two lines cut by a transversal, aimed at strengthening their understanding of the kind of angles formed when this happens.

She asks, "What do you notice about the angles inside the two parallel lines?"

"The big ones all look the same size, and the small ones all look the same size," Jason volunteered.

Figure 3.1

Transversal Extensions

1. If two lines are cut by a transversal and two of the angles formed measure 56° and 124°, explain everything that you can conclude about the eight angles formed and the relationship of the two lines to each other.

2. How can you use what you know about what happens when two parallel lines are cut by a transversal to determine the measurements of all angles in a parallelogram if you know the measurement of only one angle. Are there any other polygons that this concept can help you with determining the angle measurements? Which polygons will this concept not help with?

3. Describe everything you can about the angles formed by two lines that are not parallel when they are cut by a transversal.

"You can't trust pictures in geometry. You always need the actual measures," Tanisha reminds him.

Ms. Chou supports her, but reminds them that this is not a formal math task, just observation, and continues to prod for observations.

Sana remarks, "It looks like if you could pick up the four angles made where the transversal cuts the lower parallel line, they would fit exactly over those made by where the transversal cuts the upper parallel line."

After collecting several more observations, Ms. Chou reveals the theorems about which specific angles have equal measures within two parallel lines cut by a transversal. At this point, several students are ready to move on, while others are not yet comfortable with the topic. For those who need more exposure and practice, she offers the option of several practice problems from the text. For the two students struggling with the concept, she has them build models with pipe cleaners or wiki sticks and use protractors to ensure that the angles have the same measures as they build these models. By actually lifting the models, they can see that the angles formed at each intersection of the transversal are equal.

For those who feel they are comfortable with the lesson, she suggests they begin the extensions as well. Ms. Chou circulates, answering questions and offering assistance. When students complete the text problems and self-correct them with the key, they begin working on the extensions also. All students are then encouraged to think about the extensions for a moment.

Ms. Chou brings the whole class together to discuss the first extension question. Several students cite their peers' earlier comments about all large/small angles looking similar and the appearance that if you lifted one parallel line, its angles would fit perfectly over the other parallel line's angles. These observations helped the students recall the theorem for corresponding, alternate, and vertical angles. Other students more formally reasoned that the steps for how using the supplementary angle measures would lead them to prove that the lines must be parallel. The class then reviewed the first extension together, and one of the students who had worked on it early in the lesson walks everyone through a possible solution. A peer shares another solution, and students comment on which solution seems more efficient and which they would most likely remember and understand more easily.

Ms. Chou makes sure they all understand the homework and checks in to ensure those who are doing challenges know which to do and where to find the solutions on her class website.

WHAT IS A TIERED LESSON?

As this lesson illustrates, tiered instruction allows students to branch off at exit points (usually after lesson introduction) to take varied leveled pathways while learning about the same topics. Tiering lessons is central to formative assessment and differentiating instruction. In fact, formative assessment has recently been defined not as a tool, but rather in terms of how the data collected are actually used to alter learning and teaching, by students and teachers (Andrade, 2010). Chapter 2 focused primarily on students using the data from formative assessment. In this chapter, the focus is on teachers using the data gained from formative assessments to inform instructional adjustments they make in their teaching—largely through tiering lessons. Although definitions of the terms *tiered* and *differentiation* may have subtle differences across different theorists, I use the terms in this book in the following ways. By tiered, I am referring to leveled activities. By differentiation, I am referring to a broader picture that would include differences between tasks that are based on different interests or learning profile approaches in addition to different levels.

To foster classroom community, a tiered lesson usually begins with the same concept, then offers multiple (often three—but this is not a hard-and-fast rule) routes for students to pursue. Tiered instruction is not three separate lessons, nor does every lesson need to be tiered. Also, in many cases, only one part of the lesson is tiered. In this example, the guided and independent practice section was tiered. The purpose of tiering lessons is to better respond to the many and diverse ways that students learn best or to match instruction to student needs so that all students will move as far forward as they can, given where they each began.

This chapter provides tips for tiering lessons that are designed to be manageable and not too time-consuming. Tiering instruction can be one of the more intimidating aspects of differentiating instruction. It can seem overwhelming to plan for the different dimensions of the lesson. However, although tiering can require careful planning, it can often be done with low preparation time needed as well, as most of the examples in this chapter demonstrate. Once teachers shift from whole class planning to tiered lesson planning, they quickly find that even small adjustments along these lines can reap large learning benefits, according to self-reports from the teachers who I worked with in the focus groups in which we tested the principles in this book. Crafting the adjustments can be done slowly. Some teachers begin with just tiering one or two lessons each unit, then building up over time. Also, when formative assessments show all students have little knowledge of a new topic, then whole class teaching is appropriate until formative assessments show that students moving at a faster pace have mastered the material and require challenge.

Specific strategies for tiering lessons such as challenging all learners, minimizing task differences, and crafting open questions are discussed in this section. This is followed by sections with recommendations for how to tier a lesson by student or instructional characteristics and within a prescribed curriculum. The chapter concludes with a step-by-step format for tiering formal lessons and several model tiered lessons. These lessons demonstrate that tiering is not three separate lessons, but merely adjustments that add the supports to make tasks more easily accessible or challenges that extend the lesson to different levels. In fact, when working collaboratively with groups of math teachers to tier lessons, I often found that some of the most promising tiers involved small adjustments—just tweaking tasks to build in scaffolded supports or more complexity. Specifically, tiering most often involves adjustments made to the middle section of the lesson, the guided and independent practice sections. As the model lesson shows, this can often just mean giving one group extensions while offering support when teaching the standard level of the concept to another group. It really can be that simple. Spending time elaborately tiering lessons may not achieve much more in student learning than would a simple quick adjustment that allows students to work at their instructional level. If a teacher enjoys the creative process of tiering elaborately, then do so. But for teachers who want to guard their time, I and the teachers I have worked with have found that the simple quick tiers modeled in this chapter may often be just as effective.

Offer Challenge to All Students

As Ms. Chou's lesson demonstrates in a mixed-ability class, all students can work on similar tasks and concepts, yet at different readiness levels, designed to meet the learning needs of each student. In this lesson, students who had already known the main idea of the lesson, which was a review of vocabulary terms, worked on related challenges. In the end, these challenges were available to all students, and the building blocks needed to solve the challenges were laid down during the lesson. All students then had time to discover the solution to at least one extension, with hints offered during class so that when its solution was discussed, everyone could participate in and gain from the discussion. In this way, the classwide discussion of the same challenge problem built a cohesive community in which all students felt challenged, yet some received the additional scaffolds needed to approach the problem while others moved ahead.

Often it will take more than one lesson to get through the foundational material needed for some to be ready to tackle the challenges. For teachers with a prescribed curriculum, this can mean that they need to prioritize which tasks are less central and can be moved through more quickly to save time. During a conversation on this issue that I had with a group of teachers in a school where they used a prescribed curriculum, one teacher prodded another with questions along the lines of, "But don't you find that there are some lessons that students pick up quickly and so you can breeze through them at a faster pace and use the saved time to build in time for tiered extra support?"

Minimize Differences Between Tasks

Unless students are rotating through discrete activities at separate centers, differences between varied assignments or tasks should not result in some being universally more appealing than others. Although tasks may differ in complexity, number of facets, or level of abstraction, they should address the same concept. The purpose is not to hide differentiation. As discussed in Chapter 1, a climate should be fostered in which differences in how students learn are valued and celebrated, and so it is respected as the norm that peers will regularly work on different tasks because they have different learning profiles and needs.

Instead, teachers should strive to keep tasks as closely related as possible so that students can engage in shared discussions of material. Again, this builds a cohesive class community, yet also allows students to learn from one another. Students frequently complain when they need to listen to basic questions and answers that they have already mastered. These question-and-answer sessions should usually take place in small groups while those who are ready to can move on. The shared discussions should take place when all students have had the scaffolds and background learning to be able to engage in higher level discussions of the material. Along these lines, peer tutoring might have a place at infrequent times but can be overdone and result in some resenting that they are constantly needing to help peers rather than pursuing their own interests and challenges. I am unaware of research on the effectiveness of peer tutoring for middle school math.

Students who have mastered the basic concepts in a lesson, such as the vocabulary terms used to identify the various angles that are formed when two lines are cut by a transversal, should be allowed to work independently on challenges as the class learns these. Once the class has learned them, the entire class can have a shared discussion of more open challenging questions such as, "Given two angles that measure 116° and 64°, and that these angles are located on two lines that are cut by a transversal, how can you prove that the lines must be parallel?" In this way, students will work on the same topic, yet do so at different paces. As a caveat, one group should not be working on an exciting software task or playing a boisterous game, while other groups do text problems or worksheets, as some might resent others having more "perceived" fun. Once when Mr. Martin ran a lesson with one part involving students doing a task on the computer, that task became the favorite and all of the other students were clearly just awaiting their turn. This differs from students doing different work content because of different learning needs. Likewise, students should be given the same overall amount of work, though inevitably students who need more practice will have less time to pursue certain challenges.

Craft Open-Ended Questions

Asking open-ended questions plays a central role in a differentiated math classroom, is a powerful strategy for math differentiation (Small, 2010), and was found to be one of the most effective strategies according to the research in Black and colleagues (2003). See Small (2010) for an excellent resource on this strategy. Ideally, open-ended questions should be planned in advance as it can be challenging to come up with them spontaneously. Open-ended questions can be related to the lesson or crafted around any topic that arises in class. For example, one teacher scored a test using a 42-point scale. She then decided to give more weight to one answer, and so she changed the scale to 44. When she returned the tests, she explained this change that she had made. Since the unit was on percentages, she posed a challenge, "If you missed one point, what kind of scoring scale would give you a better score and by how much? Is there another way to do this that might be even more advantageous?" Teachers can plan for just one or two open-ended questions for each lesson to start slowly.

When crafting open-ended questions, turning an algorithm into a word problem is a formula that can frequently be used to open a question up, as word problems can often stretch students to forge deeper connections and understandings, particularly when related to real life. Similarly, transforming algorithms such as quadratic equations into diagrams can also stretch and enhance understandings. Opening up questions so that there are multiple solutions or responses can also make them more challenging and interesting, as these examples illustrate:

1.a. Single answer question—How do you solve $\frac{3}{4}$ divided by $\frac{1}{2}$?

1.b. Open-ended question—Why do you invert the second fraction when dividing fractions? Offer more than one way of explaining this.

2.a. Single answer question—What is the slope in $y = 3x + 4$?

2.b. Open-ended question—Using graph paper, draw a hill that you would like to sled down and calculate its slope. Draw a hill that a very small child could sled down, and calculate its slope. What do you notice about the two slopes?

Further questioning strategies specifically designed for math teachers that can also be used during any lesson to take the discussion to varied levels are available at:

http//:teacherline.pbs.org/teacherline/resources/questionsheet_vma.pdf. To design questions, Benjamin Bloom's classic framework can be used, and words can be drawn from charts, such as the following, which are available on the Internet.

Designing Questions	
Category	**Example and Key Words**
Knowledge: Recall data or information.	**Key Words:** Define, describe, identify, know, label, list, match, name, outline, recall, recognize, reproduce, select, state
Comprehension: Understand the meaning, translation, interpolation, and interpretation of instructions and problems. State a problem in one's own words.	**Key Words:** Comprehend, convert, defend, distinguish, estimate, explain, extend, generalize, give examples, infer, interpret, paraphrase, predict, rewrite, summarize, translate
Application: Use a concept in a new situation or unprompted use of an abstraction. Applies what was learned in the classroom into novel situations in the work place.	**Key Words:** Apply, change, compute, construct, demonstrate, discover, manipulate, modify, operate, predict, prepare, produce, relate, show, solve, use
Analysis: Separates material or concepts into component parts so that its organizational structure may be understood. Distinguishes between facts and inferences.	**Key Words:** Analyze, break down, compare, contrast, diagram, deconstruct, differentiate, discriminate, distinguish, identify, illustrates, infer, outline, relate, select, separate
Synthesis: Builds a structure or pattern from diverse elements. Put parts together to form a whole, with emphasis on creating a new meaning or structure.	**Key Words:** Categorize, combine, compile, compose, create, devise, design, explain, generate, modify, organize, plan, rearrange, reconstruct, relate, reorganize, revise, rewrite, summarize, tell, write
Evaluation: Make judgments about the value of ideas or materials.	**Key Words:** Appraise, compare, conclude, contrast, criticize, critique, defend, describe, discriminate, evaluate, explain, interpret, justify, relate, summarize, support
See: http://www.nwlink.com/~donclark/hrd/bloom.html, where this chart and more useful resources are posted.	

Ultimately students should be coached to ask higher level questions themselves. To scaffold this, teachers can use question starters and have students practice writing questions they have for each topic on homework, in class, or during discussions. To really hone the skill, teachers could model good questions, then have students create questions and score them with rubrics that detail what makes the question good.

As an extension of open-ended questions, students should also be given opportunities to engage in open-ended tasks. For example, students who complete problems on graphing linear relationships could hunt for linear relationships in real life and present some counter examples as well; they could explore whether jumping jacks and elapsed time are a linear relationship or whether the height of a pile and the corresponding number of stacking cups that compose the pile are linearly related. They can also look at graphs of slopes and compare their steepness with actual models such as how quickly a stack of books grows when four books are added each time versus when two are added, and how this looks when graphed—and what effect it has on the slope in the equation. They could use evidence from such examples to then reflect more meaningfully in their journals on the question "What is a linear relationship?"

DIFFERENTIATING BY STUDENT CHARACTERISTICS

As a framework for how to tier a math lesson, teachers can think about whether they want to differentiate first according to student characteristics, which include readiness, interests, and learning profiles.

Readiness

6 | **Data-Informed Instruction**

Lessons can be differentiated by readiness based on preassessment results. The most solid research base supports tiering by readiness. In a large-scale research study, Tieso (2005) studied the effects of tiering math instruction by readiness with 645 students. First, students took a diagnostic preassessment, then were grouped according to readiness and taught differentiated curricula. They made significantly greater progress in comparison to control students who were not taught according to readiness.

One model for thinking about how to tier by readiness is Carol Ann Tomlinson's "Equalizer" (1999). In this model, attributes of the lesson are viewed as knobs on a stereo that can be adjusted one way or another to increase or decrease the challenge level of a task. The following are traits that can be adjusted on their respective continua on which a task can fall.

The Task-Planning "Equalizer"

Foundational..Transformational

Concrete..Abstract

Simple..Complex

Single Facet..Multifaceted

More Structured..More Open

Clearly Defined ....Fuzzy Problem

Less Independence..More Independence

Slower..Quicker Pace

Foundational tasks lay the building blocks (vocabulary, procedures, basic concepts) for students to then do more transformational tasks in which information is manipulated or thought about in a new way. Concrete tasks are more tangible tasks, frequently those that use manipulatives that can be seen and touched, while abstract tasks require more mental stamina and leaps. Simple tasks can be solved in a straightforward way while complex tasks require grasping a more challenging concept. A single-facet task implies one step, and multifaceted tasks require more steps and connections. All steps are provided in a structured problem, and there is usually one defined solution. With open tasks, students can make more choices, research alternatives, and determine which angle they prefer and state why. Fuzzy problems have no defined solutions, so they can be taken to various levels. More steps are needed for planning and monitoring how to carry out a task that can be done with greater independence. Finally, tasks can be adjusted for the pace at which they are to be solved. In the opening lesson, Ms. Chou's extensions involved students moving at a faster pace, while the full class lesson on vocabulary moved at a slower pace.

The following are examples of different kinds of activities that might fall under the varied continua:

- Foundational—draw at least five possible nets for a cube.
- Transformational—most cube nets have six pieces. Can you make a cube net with nine pieces? More than nine? (Think of using triangles.)

- Concrete—list the number of faces on a cube and on a triangular prism. Draw the net.
- Abstract—draw a 3-D shape with five faces, then seven. Draw the net. Is there another way to draw them?

- Simple—find the volume of a soup can and list the steps to do so.
- Complex—is the ratio of a soup can's volume to another with twice the height but the same radius more or less economical than one with the same height but twice the radius?

- Single facet—find the volume of a rectangular prism.
- Multifacet—find the volume of an irregularly shaped prism.

- More structure—what is the total surface area of an 8-oz. juice box and an 8-oz. soda can?
- More open—design a beverage holder for a hiker. Tell its surface area and volume, and explain the advantages of why you constructed it for the hiker in the way that you did.

- Clearly defined—draw a net of a given solid.
- Fuzzy problem—draw a net of a solid in which the number of shapes in the net outnumber the number of faces on the solid. What is the biggest gap you can design?

Interests

Lessons can also be differentiated by interests. Although there is not as much research on tiering by interest, I, as well as the teachers I have worked with, have found that it uplifts motivation and is beneficial for class climate. When students are interested in material, they persevere more. Also, interests often give clues as to where child is cognitively and developmentally.

When doing a unit on probability, students who play basketball can easily grasp the probabilities of one-on-one or two-shot free throws, though they may struggle with equally abstract concepts that they cannot relate to as well. Similarly, I have seen shifts in understanding when teaching linear equations through car rentals, which students cannot relate to, and then through cell phone plan options, which students can relate to. Figure 3.2 shows an interest survey teachers can collect and refer to when brainstorming tasks or option menus. In order not to lose instructional time, the survey could be completed for homework. Collecting and compiling this information can be time-consuming and is not recommended. Students could do this at a learning center activity as a data analysis project if they finish their work early. Otherwise, teachers can simply keep these papers in a folder and skim through them when thinking about ideas for topics that will be interesting to students. They really need not be formally compiled, as this is not a good use of time or necessary.

Figure 3.2

Interest Profile

List your specific interests in the following categories:

Music: List your favorite songs, artists, groups, instruments, or musical genre (i.e., rock, jazz, hip-hop).

Clothing: List your favorite clothing.

Shopping: What kinds of things do you like to shop for?

Sports: List sports you like to watch and/or play.

Social avenues: Describe your preferred social avenues and how much time you spend on each (cell phones, Facebook).

Entertainment: Describe your favorite movies, television, YouTube.

Hobbies or activities: What are your favorites?

List any other interests.

Learning Profiles

Alternatively, lessons can be differentiated according to various models for assessing learning profiles or preferences. Interestingly, the literature on differentiating instruction uses the term *learning profile*. Learning style is typically associated with models such as VAK (visual-auditory-kinesthetic). However, though much research has been done, it has yet to substantiate that matching instruction to learning styles uplifts achievement (Krätzig & Arbuthnott, 2006). Also, I have also heard it advised that students should not be taught according to one style, but teachers should strengthen all three. *Learning profile* broadens the term to include models such as Mel Levine's eight neurodevelopmental constructs (Scherer, 2006).

Levine's Neurodevelopmental Constructs

Levine profiles an individual's strengths and weaknesses on the basis of eight neurodevelopmental constructs. Below are a few of the subskills included in each construct.

Attention. *Alertness, mental effort, saliency determination, focus maintenance, facilitation, inhibition, pacing, self-monitoring.*

Temporal Sequential Ordering. *Sequential perception and memory, time management.*

Spatial Ordering. *Spatial awareness and perception, materials management.*

Memory. *Short-term, active, and long-term memory; memory access and consolidation.*

Language. *Phonological processing, sentence comprehension, articulation and fluency, semantic use, word retrieval, verbal elaboration.*

Neuromotor Functions. *Gross motor, fine motor, and graphomotor functions.*

Social Cognition. *Communication, conversational technique, humor regulation, self-marketing, collaboration, conflict resolution, political acumen.*

Higher Order Cognition. *Concept formation, critical thinking, creativity, problem-solving, reasoning, logical thinking, mental representation.*

Source: Scherer, 2006.

Admittedly, there has been controversy surrounding the fact that there has not yet been enough research on using this approach. However, I, as well as many of the teachers I know, have found this a useful framework for thinking about individual student profiles. Teachers can use this framework to pinpoint varied strengths and difficulties, then to adjust lessons to play to student strengths. For example, I had one student who had weak language, memory, and attentional skills, but strong higher order thinking skills. He responded well to practicing skills that he needed to develop in the context of a challenge problem that intrigued him. Another student struggled with all of these issues as well, but she had strong social cognitive skills, and so I had her work with peers as often as possible. A third student had strong sequential skills, in that she could

Differentiation of Student Work 7

work step-by-step in an organized way easily. She also had strong language skills but severely impaired visual spatial skills. Therefore, I had her write out all of the steps to visual problems in sentences, written right next to the visual images. Many models exist for understanding various learning profiles. Mel Levine's merely appeals to me and many of the teachers I know as one of the clearer and more comprehensive ones. I have found it tremendously helpful as a lens for breaking down how each child approaches learning, and then using that to make teaching adjustments.

Many inventories of learning profiles are available online. Students could fill one out at home or during a computer class. When done online, the results are instantly tallied and analyzed, and so it is advisable to do them online. Teachers could ask for printouts, and students can summarize what they learn about themselves and how this applies to math class in a brief summary that they turn in a homework packet. Mel Levine's website www.allkindsofminds.org offers abundant suggestions, resources, and strategies for addressing learning profiles, and those at this site claim they are currently conducting and collating research on these, which is available at the website. Again, this is not a research-based strategy but looks promising in terms of developing metacognitive self-directedness.

TIERING BY INSTRUCTIONAL CHARACTERISTICS

Additionally or alternatively, lessons can be differentiated according to instructional characteristics, which include content, processes, and products.

Content

⑦ Differentiation of Student Work

When tiering content, students engage in the same type of work, but the content they work on is adjusted. ⑦ For example, students in Ms. Musambee's class each completed a project in which they learned new geometry vocabulary terms. Those students who had shown that they already knew most of the terms were given more complicated terms for their projects. In the end, they all created projects that looked similar; however, upon closer examination, some of the projects had more complex vocabulary terms.

As another example, when teaching students to graph slopes, students who finish early can then identify varying levels of patterns in different groups of equations, as in an activity in which they are given linear equations to plot on graphs (see Figure 3.3). Students who master the content quickly could look for how the direction or steepness of the line is influenced when the slope is negative or a fraction, which is the focus of the first set. The focus of the second set is simplified, in that the difference between Y-intercepts are positive and negative. To vary the format for Figure 3.3, the following cards could be printed on business card stock, laminated, cut into individual cards and passed out to the students. In the two sets of problems that are given in Figure 3.3, both cover the same content material, yet in one set the content is more advanced. Students can then do a variation of card sorts once they have graphed the lines. In this activity, students then sort the cards based on similar pattern. Students could then reflect on the patterns they see, why they are there, what is the rule, and why the rule works, then share insights in a full class discussion. This activity can also be done with graphing calculators.

Figure 3.3

Graphing Linear Equations

Positive/Negative Slope

$y = \dfrac{2}{3}x + 7$ $\qquad\qquad$ $y = \dfrac{3}{4}x + 2$

$y = \dfrac{1}{3}x + 4$ $\qquad\qquad$ $y = \dfrac{3}{5}x + 6$

$y = \dfrac{1}{2}x + 4$ $\qquad\qquad$ $y = \dfrac{1}{3}x + 4$

$y = \dfrac{1}{4}x + 2$ $\qquad\qquad$ $y = -\dfrac{3}{5}x + 2$

Positive/Negative Y-Intercept

$y = 3x - 7$ $\qquad\qquad$ $y = 4x + 2$

$y = 3x - 4$ $\qquad\qquad$ $y = 5x + 6$

$y = x + 4$ $\qquad\qquad$ $y = x - 4$

$y = 4x + 2$ $\qquad\qquad$ $y = 5x + 2$

As an example of how to tier content with low preparation time needed, Ms. Musambee once gave a quiz and found students made errors that fit into four categories. Instead of moving ahead, she chose to use the quiz as a powerful formative assessment, in that it informed both her instructional adjustments and her students' decisions and the next steps they took about what they needed to learn. In her words:

Differentiation of Student Work **7**

So, I did something today that's a good example of last-minute differentiation (not totally "on the fly," but not planned way in advance either). As I was correcting students' quizzes last night (on multiplying fractions, mixed numbers, and decimals), I noticed there were many students making procedural errors. After looking at them all, I realized students fell into four general categories: the students who made no mistakes or only

> *calculation errors, the ones who made many errors multiplying decimals (either on their multiplication or on their placement of the decimal point), the ones who needed practice multiplying fractions by whole numbers, and the ones who needed help multiplying mixed numbers. Before the students came in, I found different sheets for students to choose from: one to practice multiplying mixed numbers, one to practice whole numbers times fractions, one to practice multiplying decimals, and one integer extension. In class, I told them about the results of the quiz and chose one of each type of problem to go over. Then I told students the options they had, and I had them choose the sheet to work on during class. Kids chose very well, and when I checked in with them at the end, they felt much more secure and confident with the procedure they had worked on.*

This example demonstrates how quickly and easily lessons can be differentiated. It is really more about a shift in mindset while planning than an additional time commitment. But what if students do not choose well and choose a group with friends or a too easy task? Once a self-directed climate is fostered, this is less likely to occur. Teachers can also approve or not approve choices.

Processes

Lessons can also be differentiated according to the different processes students will use to achieve the same curricular goals. Frameworks such as Howard Gardner's (1983) multiple intelligences can be used to tier assignments or tasks according to different processes. The following is a list of these eight intelligences:

- Linguistic intelligence (word smart)
- Logical-mathematical intelligence (number/reasoning smart)
- Spatial intelligence (picture smart)
- Bodily-kinesthetic intelligence (body smart)
- Musical intelligence (music smart)
- Interpersonal intelligence (people smart)
- Intrapersonal intelligence (self-smart)
- Naturalist intelligence (nature smart)

Lessons might be differentiated by the process of how students learn, such as tiering lessons in geometry through songs they write (musical intelligence) or through acting out with their bodies (bodily intelligence) various vocabulary terms in a geometry lesson. Likewise, students could learn to distinguish between various groups of polygons through categorizing them within a Venn diagram (logical-mathematical), through cutting them out (kinesthetic), or sorting them into various groups and defending (word smart) why each is placed in its group.

As an example, students may benefit from learning through movement because of weak conceptual understandings that can be compensated for through alternate routes; for example, one student I taught seemed to have a weak mental structure of a number line in her mind, which made adding and subtracting integers challenging for her. Gersten and Chard (1999) cite research suggesting that this mental number line may be a critical big idea for understanding these kinds of fundamental concepts in mathematics. I once put a piece of tape on the floor and numbered it with positive and negative integers. She walked on this line whenever she had to solve an integers problem. Once I saw her taking a test and her back was swaying forward and backward ever so slightly as she solved the problems correctly.

Another student used kinesthetic or bodily intelligence to help her recall the concepts associated with point, line segment, ray, and line. For point, she decided to create a fist. For line segment, she extended both arms outward perpendicularly and made two fists. For ray, she did the same, but created one fist and with her other hand extended her fingers outwards. For line, she extended both arms and all fingers on both hands. She later taught this to her class and excelled on the unit test. Both of these cases dramatically illustrate the potential power of differentiating instruction in making mathematics not only more challenging but also more accessible for all types of learners.

Differentiation of Student Work **7**

Final Products

Similarly, students can master objectives through different products. Some students might write a brief report describing various groups of polygons and why they would fall into separate categories, while others might create a poster conveying this information. The big idea is that the product is not the end goal, but mastering the standard. For example, when teaching students to master a concept, they could choose from items in a standard menu to complete varied final products (see Figure 3.4).

Figure 3.4

Menu of Product Options

Select one option from the menu below to represent your understanding of the current topic. The project will be scored on the accuracy, clarity, and completeness of the explanation of the math topic, as well as the quality of the presentation of the material.

Poster	Song or Poem
Design a poster that conveys the concept with clear diagrams, steps of the process, and other images that showed deep understanding of the concept.	Write a song, rap song, or poem that explains the concept and all the steps needed to solve it.
3-D Image	**Written Explanation**
Design a 3-D image and a diorama-type box that represents the concept and the steps of the process involved in the concept.	Write a one-page explanation of the global concept and all of the steps needed to show the concept being accurately performed.

Defining *quality of presentation* can be subjective, so adding more detail, or having students add this detail, may be important.

TIERING EXISTING TEXTBOOK LESSONS

Many math teachers claim that they must adhere to a prescribed curriculum as it is laid out in their textbooks. Fortunately, the teacher's guides for most textbooks usually offer abundant ways to tier lessons. Owning a few alternative textbooks can provide a wealth of additional strategies and activities for differentiating instruction at one's finger tips, all arranged by specific math topics for easy reference. Publishers will usually give sample text books for free, and they can also be purchased online at significant discount.

Reteaching, practice, and enrichment worksheets are usually available with most textbook collections. After teaching an introductory mini lesson on a specific topic, a brief assessment can be used to create exit points in which a teacher can then distribute these three types of sheets based on student performance. The reteaching sheets can be supplemented with the learning strategies described in Chapter 4 so that these students are not merely receiving more of the same, but the information is offered in different ways that may better meet their learning needs.

The practice sheets can be compacted, in the sense that they can be made shorter with unnecessary repetitive material removed, so that students have the option of completing the most challenging problems first and looping out of the assignment if it is too easy for them and move into the enrichment sheets. Chapter 5 provides an evaluative criterion that can be used to judge the appropriateness of the enrichment activities. Most of these activities are designed to branch out rather than move students ahead in the curricular sequence, which is preferred in some schools.

CREATING A DIFFERENTIATED LESSON

The first step to creating a differentiated lesson is to clarify the lesson standard that all students are expected to master. For Ms. Chou, this was identifying all angles formed when two parallel lines are cut by a transversal. Prerequisite skills should also be listed and assessed. For this lesson, the vocabulary terms were the prerequisites (i.e., parallel lines, complementary angles). When teaching students to graph slopes, teachers should check for prerequisites such as students' ability to plot points on a graph. Students can be preassessed on a formal preassessment given at the start of the unit and/or again when the lesson begins. Common misconceptions should be planned for in advance, and strategies for addressing them prepared.

Next, plan for a lesson introduction that will activate background knowledge, enable students to connect what they are learning to what they already know, and captivate their interest. In the opening lesson, Ms. Chou, at one point, asked students to write what they notice about the parallel lines and the transversal, an open question with no right or wrong response that achieved these objectives. Opening up questions can often make them more motivating. Next, plan whether to tier content, process, or product and by readiness, interest, or learning profile. In this case, Ms. Chou differentiated by readiness, and gave a more abstract, advanced challenge to those who were ready. Most students picked up the concept as they did guided problems. A few needed to build models with pipe cleaners and see concretely how actually picking up one set of angles and placing them over the other set of angles confirms that both sets of angles are in fact equal. Lessons should generally open together, then branch off into different tiers, and then reconvene at the end, as the lesson by Ms. Chou demonstrates. If time does not allow for this, students who did not do the challenges in class could do them for homework, and the full class can discuss them the next day. As students demonstrate mastery or show a need for additional instruction, teachers need to have activities on hand and ready for use as well as independent practice. These can be a page of extensions (as in Figure 3.1), a packet of related extensions, or an in-depth task. The lesson should always conclude with some type of assessment so that student learning can be evaluated, ideally by students themselves, with an element of feedback included. Figure 3.5 is a format for how to design a differentiated lesson, followed by five sample lesson plans that demonstrate how a teacher might tier a lesson (see Figures 3.6–3.10).

Figure 3.5

Format for Tiering Lessons

Unit Topic/Specific Standard All Should Master:

    Preassessment data/Predictable misconceptions or progressions

Motivation/Introduction—activate background knowledge

    Formative assessment: What tasks will reveal which students can bypass to extensions?

    Lesson steps/Differentiated independent practice—scaffolds/extensions

    All class discussion topic/Challenge

    Assessment

    Homework

Figure 3.6

Tiered Lesson

Exponents

National Council of Teachers of Mathematics (NCTM) Content Standard: Numbers and Operations

Objective: Knows difference between multiplicative and exponential growth.

Preassessment: List students whose preassessments show they have mastered the topic.

Motivation/Introduction

1. Distribute cubes: 100 small soft squares (1 cm or smaller).

2. Write on the board $4 + 4 + 4$ and tell students to represent this with cubes. What does this mean? Is there a shorter way to write it? Why was multiplication invented? (Mathematicians love to find shorter ways to express mathematical ideas.)

3. Write on the board $4 \times 4 \times 4$. Tell students to represent it. Provide differentiated levels of support, as needed.
   ○ Ask: What does this mean? Do you think there might be a shorter way to write this? Have all students record their ideas and share them in small groups or pairs.

Formative assessment—If it becomes apparent that any students know exponents, they should move on to the extensions.

Lesson steps:

1. Ensure students understand the convention of exponents. Multiplication is just repeated addition; similarly, exponents are a way to express simply repeated multiplication.

2. Have students build with manipulatives models of 4×3 and 4^3. What do they notice? In sentences, have them write the difference between standard multiplication and exponents. (Examples: The exponent is actually stronger than multiplication. Multiplication is another way of doing addition. Exponents are another way of doing multiplication. Repeated addition and repeated multiplication are the differences.)

Supports/Tiered practice: Have students practice building several more (e.g., 3×4 and 3^4) and drawing what they have built. When the majority of the class is getting them correct (20 problems or until 85% accuracy is achieved), move ahead to challenges. Those students who need more practice with manipulatives should continue building models and be guided to begin drawing representations.

Extensions/Tiered practice: Distribute challenges attached to this lesson.

All class discussion: Discuss the first challenge.

Assessment: Have students self-correct their work and comment on how comfortable they are with this topic.

Homework: Have students do problems from text or challenges, based on comfort with this lesson, with teacher input.

Exponents Lesson Full Class Worksheet:

Build both 4×3 and 4^3 What do you notice? How are they different?

What is the difference between standard multiplication and exponents?

How would you define each: standard multiplication and exponents?

Write $4 \times 4 \times 4$ using exponents:

Write 7^3 as standard multiplication:

Each of these are written in exponential form. Write them in standard form (draw models and show work):

7^3	5^4	6^2
4^3	8^4	2^3
9^2	6^4	5^3

What is your plan for remembering the difference between multiplication and exponents?

Write it in poem form.

(Continued)

(Continued)

Exponents Lesson Extensions

1. How many ways can you represent 64 with exponents?

2. Explain why 4 squared is called squared? Why is 4 cubed called cubed?

3. Why do you think a number raised to the 0 power is always 1?

4. When 0 is raised to the power of 0, the answer is undefined. Take a side and argue it.

5. If exponents represent repeated multiplication, what would represent repeated exponents? Design a system.

Figure 3.7

Tiered Lesson

Scale Factor

NCTM Content Standard: Measurement

Scale Factor Investigation Lab

Standard: Discover what happens when you dilate figures by a factor that is less than 1 and greater than 1.

Preassessment: Have students define key vocabulary terms and concepts such as dilation, reduction, enlargement, and scale factor. Those who know the terms and concept of dilating by greater/less than 1 move ahead to challenges.

Motivation/Introduction:

When in life would you need to make a smaller or larger model of an object? (Architects)

When designing a school, if the perimeter of the building is 50 m $\times$ 75 m, what would be a reasonable smaller scale model size? Have all students write their answers. Share a few. Collect and use these as an assessment as well. (5 $\times$ 7.5?)

Review terms. Practice reducing rectangles.

Lesson steps: Carry out attached math lab to discover what happens when you dilate (make smaller or larger) a figure by a scale factor less than 1 or greater than 1.

Students write pattern that they see in their journals.

Lab Answers:

Dilate a rectangle that is 2 cm $\times$ 4 cm using a scale factor of 2.5 (5 cm $\times$ 10 cm).

Dilate a triangle that is 6″ $\times$ 8″ $\times$ 10″ by a scale factor of 4.5 (27″ $\times$ 36″ $\times$ 45″).

Dilate a theater that is 9′ $\times$ 6′ by a scale factor of $\frac{1}{10}$ so that you can build a model of it ($\frac{9}{10} \times \frac{3}{5}$).

Dilate a rectangle that is 15″ $\times$ 25″ by a scale factor of $\frac{1}{5}$ (3″ $\times$ 5″).

Have students create diagrams for each figure.

Tiered Guided Practice (Differentiated by readiness and interest):

1. Extension—Students who did not test out of the lesson with a preassessment, but then master the lesson quickly are exempt from creating diagrams. They can then dilate common objects they have such as pencil cases. As a further activity or a menu item, they can also build scale models of their bedrooms or classroom.

2. Support—Students who are not mastering the concept can meet in a small group and learn a diagramming strategy that they can later teach to the larger class. They can also use this strategy to build scale models of their bedrooms or classroom.

Assessment/Class discussion: Discuss the first extension on maps and use this as an assessment of where students are at.

Homework: Students use teacher input to help them decide whether to complete text problems or extensions.

(Continued)

(Continued)

Scale Factor Lesson Plan Worksheet

Diagram each:

Dilate these rectangles by a scale factor of 5.

Dilate a rectangle that is 2 cm $\times$ 4 cm using a scale factor of 2.5.

Dilate a triangle that is 6″ $\times$ 8″ $\times$ 10″ by a scale factor of 4.5.

Dilate a theater that is 9′ $\times$ 6′ by a scale factor of $\frac{1}{10}$ so that you can build a model of it.

Dilate a rectangle that is 15″ $\times$ 25″ by a scale factor of $\frac{1}{5}$.

Write each solution in the chart below depending on whether it was dilated by a factor that is less than or greater than 1:

Larger Than One	Less Than One

What pattern do you notice?

Scale Factor Extensions

1. A map uses a scale factor of $\frac{3}{4}$ cm equals 40 miles. If the distance between two cities is $4\frac{1}{2}$ centimeters, how many miles is it? Would this be a reasonable scale to represent the distance between New York City and Boston? Between New York City and Los Angeles? Why or why not?

2. Design a reasonable scale factor for representing the distance between New York City and Los Angeles. Design one for measuring the distance between Boston and New York City. Between Moscow and New Delhi.

3. Choose a rectangular object and enlarge it by a scale factor of 4. What happens to the volume and the area on the outside faces of the object?

Figure 3.8

Tiered Lesson

Angles in a Triangle

NCTM Content Standard: Geometry

Objective: Learn that the interior angles in a triangle equal 180°.

Preassessment: Ensure that all students know how to use a protractor and can measure angles. List any students who already know the concept as indicated on preassessment.

Motivation: Post a large triangle. Have students in the class estimate what the measure of each angle inside the triangle is. Then have them add up the estimated measurements.

Steps: Have student cut out a triangle from card stock. Then have them tear off corners (do not cut them off). Then, line up each corner with each point (across from tear) together so that the three pieces together create a straight 180° line.

Differentiated practice: Differentiated by learning profiles.

- For students who instantly understand that all three angles will always sum to 180°, have them practice finding the missing angle measurement in a triangle in which two angle measures are given. They can then investigate side lengths in relation to angle measures and what happens if the sum of two sides is smaller than the third.
- Students who learn best from pattern seeking can complete the lab activities.
- Additional support—Students who benefit from an alternate presentation of the same concept can try this second activity: Fold the triangle in half and put a small mark on the half-point. Open it up and fold all three corners into the half-point center. This again will show that it forms a straight line.
- Interpersonal learners can write an explanation of this process on paper to someone who cannot see.

Assessments/Class Discussion of extension

Have students write in journal: How many angles are in a triangle? What would happen to the shape if the angles measured more or less than 180°?

Homework: Have students practice finding the missing angle measurement in a triangle in which two angle measures are given.

Angles in a Triangle Lesson Plan Worksheet

In groups: Cut out five card stock triangles. Label each angle as 1, 2, or 3.

Record each angle measures here. Then add them up for each angle.

Triangle # 1

    Angle 1 =

    Angle 2 =

    Angle 3 =

    Total =

Triangle # 2

    Angle 1 =

    Angle 2 =

    Angle 3 =

    Total =

Triangle # 3

    Angle 1 =

    Angle 2 =

    Angle 3 =

    Total =

Triangle # 4

    Angle 1 =

    Angle 2 =

    Angle 3 =

    Total =

Triangle # 5

    Angle 1 =

    Angle 2 =

    Angle 3 =

    Total =

What pattern do you see?

(Continued)

(Continued)

Interior Angles Extensions

1. What would happen to a triangle if the angle measurements were less than 180° in total? More than 180°?

2. If you know the angles inside a triangle, can you insert one line through the triangle to create two new triangles in which you could find new measures of every angle, without a protractor? How many different ways could you draw the line?

3. If you know the angles in a triangle and you fold it exactly in half (if it has a line of symmetry), can you find all the angles in the new triangle? Draw it and justify your reasoning.

Figure 3.9

Tiered Lesson

Volume of Cone and Pyramid

NCTM Content Standard: Measurement

Objective: Discover formula for finding the volume of solids: cone and pyramid.

Assessment: Review key vocabulary terms. Ensure all students have mastered the formula for calculating the volume of a cylinder and cube. Those students who know how to find the volume of a cone and pyramid can do the extensions.

Materials: Plastic rice or small objects, cone and same height, same width cylinder; pyramid and same height, same width cube. Geometric Solids (Classroom Products, 888-271-8305)

Motivation/introduction

Using the manipulatives above, have students fill the cone with plastic rice.

Write a prediction: How many times does one need to do this to fill the cylinder?

Lesson steps: Then have students pour the rice into the same height/width cylinder. Count how many times it needs to be filled with rice from the cone with the same height and circumference.

Repeat this activity with the pyramid and the matching cube. Record the results and discover the formulas for these solids.

Guided Practice: Have students write out the steps for calculating the volume of cone and pyramid, and complete problems for calculating volume of these shapes.

Differentiated menu items for independent practice: Differentiated by multiple intelligences. Have students do the following:

- Write a song or poem for calculating the volume of these solids.
- Create a checklist of steps for solving such problems.
- Create a strategy that uses a mnemonic to cue the steps needed to do this.

Assessments

Have students review predictions above and make any corrections.

Give a mini quiz—Write out the steps for calculating volume of cones or pyramids. Have students reflect on the menu item chosen for learning the steps. Was it an effective method?

Whole class discussion: discuss the projects and display them.

Homework:

Have students rewrite the steps, if needed; complete 20 practice examples.

(Continued)

(Continued)

Volume of Cone and Pyramid Whole Class Activity

Estimate how many times you will need to fill the cone and empty it into the cylinder in order for the cylinder to be full.

Now perform the experiment and write your solution here.

Repeat this activity with the pyramid and the rectangular prism.

What does this tell you about the formula for finding the volume of a cone or pyramid?

Practice finding the volume of the cones and pyramids in your textbook.

Volume Extensions

1. Thinking about this activity, what can you tell me about what the volume of the sphere might be?

2. Using a rough estimate for finding the volume of a sphere, what size would a cup need to be to mean that you would get more ice cream in a cup than in a 6-in. cone if the diameter were 2.5 in.?

3. Research the actual formula for finding the volume of the sphere. Explain why the formula makes sense given what you know about cones and pyramids.

Figure 3.10

Tiered Lesson

Circumference of a Circle

NCTM Content Standard: Measurement

Objective: Visually discover the relationship between Pi and the formula for the circumference of a circle.

Preassessment: If students know the formula for calculating the circumference, they must be able to explain why it works to be exempt from this lesson.

Materials: String, scissors, cans, freezer tape, pencils, bike tire

Motivation/Introduction:

Have students draw a circle or use a can or any round object.

Measure a string across the diameter of the circle, can, or round object. Cut the string so that it goes across at the widest part of the circle. Explain that this is the diameter.

Predict: How many times would this string go around the circle?

Lesson steps: Then have students count how many times that piece of string goes around the entire circle/can.

Do 3 to 4 objects and record results.

Share these with class.

Supports—Extensions for students who do not master this formula quickly.

Put freezer tape rolled out on the desk. Roll a can beginning and ending at the same point on the can. Mark off where the can begins and ends. Then place the cans diameter across the tape as many times as it will go—note that it fits just over three times. For fun, this can be done with a large bicycle tire in the classroom also.

Do several more examples with string and small circles at their seats. Practice visualizing mentally and diagramming what they just did. Create a checklist of formula steps. Do a worksheet of practice problems and justify reasonableness of each solution.

Extension: Have students use standard and metric measuring systems to measure the distance around a circle and across the circle. Set up a ratio. Discover that no matter what measuring system is used, the ratio will be constant. If the group requiring support is using the bike tire, this group should also use a bike tire, as one object to do this. This way it does not appear that one group is doing an activity that is more exciting than the other.

Assessments: Give a mini quiz on calculating the circumference of a circle.

Homework:

Extension: A circle has a diameter of 12. If you shrink it by $\frac{1}{4}$ so that the area is now $\frac{1}{4}$ as big, what will the new diameter be?

Support: Write out an explanation of this experiment for a person who cannot see and must visualize it. Practice reading this to someone else and see if he or she can arrive at correct answers based on your description. Evaluate whether your description is thorough and accurate.

Finding Circumference of a Circle

1. Cut a piece of string that fits across the center (diameter) of a circle.

2. Estimate how many times the string will go around the circle here: _____

3. Now put the string around the circle. Make hashmarks at each place in the circle where the string ends and begins again.

4. How many times did the string go around? _____

5. Repeat this with three more circular objects and list how many times the string goes around each: _____

6. Additional practice: Take a piece of freezer tape and mark a line where the tape begins on the roll. Roll out one piece and stop at the mark. The one piece you have rolled out should be a full diameter of the roll of tape. Now put the tape roll sideways at the start of the line of the tape. Count how many times the roll of tape goes along the piece of tape that goes across your desk. What does this show?

Extensions

A circular plate fits exactly on a square tray. If the diameter of the set is 8 inches, if you roll the plate one roll along the edge of the tray, how far will it get around the tray?

If a 2-ft.-diameter bike tire can last for 100,000 ft., how much longer will a tire that is 3 ft. long in diameter last than a tire that is 2 ft. long in diameter?

4

Supporting Students Who Are Low Achieving

Each student who enters our classroom is a mystery with a uniquely varied learning profile. Uncovering how each child thinks and feels about mathematics is one of the most fulfilling and rewarding opportunities we have as teachers. Among those students with identified learning challenges, no two are ever the same, though some may share certain similar learning patterns such as difficulty with efficient and organized thinking or trouble retrieving what they know (Swanson & Deshler, 2003). However, two students diagnosed with attentional and memory difficulties may have entirely different readiness skills in different areas of math. Although familiarity with each child's learning profile is valuable, it is equally important to know simply what each child can and cannot do for each specific math unit because our preconceptions about their diagnosed difficulties may bias us, and students often surprise us in wonderful and unexpected ways.

Since the varying units, such as algebra versus geometry, draw on diverse underlying capabilities (symbolic thinking, language skill, or visual reasoning), students need opportunities, such as diagnostic preassessments and continuous formative assessments, to show what they have and have not yet mastered before and during each separate unit. Then based on what teachers learn from these assessments, differentiated content supports can be offered to address students' learning needs and to help them be more strategic in how they learn overall. However, some students with more severe gaps or learning challenges will require more than the kinds of adjustments recommended so far. In a sense, we may need to intensify our efforts to differentiate how we teach them. Although differentiation is intensified in this chapter, the emphasis remains on promoting self-direction and having students participate in directing the next steps needed for their learning as much as they can. One caveat to keep in mind throughout this chapter and book is that not all students may fully master all unit essential learnings with the same depth, but attaining a level of proficiency on each of these should always be the goal.

Beyond addressing differences in readiness levels for each specific unit, as discussed in the previous chapters, teachers can intensify how they differentiate support for the underlying, more serious difficulties students may have in three areas:

- Basic facts
- Concepts
- Procedures

Response to Intervention Tier II Interventions Described in This Chapter

Basic Facts:

- Preassess facts to develop a systematic list to address.
- If facts are known but recalled slowly, use speeded retrieval interventions.
- To build basic fact conceptual knowledge, use decomposition and arrays interventions.
- Use explicit and systematic instruction.

Conceptual Knowledge:

- Clarify difficulty first to pinpoint precise breakdown to address.
- Manipulatives: Concrete-representational-abstract learning sequence (CRA).
- Present information in graphic organizers.
- Directly teach diagramming techniques.
- Coresearch alternative explanations.

Procedures:

- Preassess procedures to develop systematic list to address.
- Use distributed practice over time rather than massed practice at once.
- Have students create checklists of procedural steps.
- Teach heuristics.
- Design strategies.

DIFFERENTIATING INSTRUCTION IN BASIC FACTS

Beverly knows her basic facts but recalls them slowly. She dreads being asked in front of the class to work out problems because she's even slower to recall them when anxious. Steven, on the other hand, never quite mastered the basic facts. Solving 6 × 7 can take a few minutes as he laboriously adds up seven 6s. Both of them have trouble with longer calculations because they cannot pull up their basic facts quickly.

By middle school, students particularly dislike drilling basic facts. However, research suggests it is critical that they know and do these effortlessly, to free up their mental resources, organize and monitor their thinking, and focus on the higher order aspects of middle school math (Delazar et al., 2003). This may also be important if students are not given certain kinds of accommodations. Teachers do need to advocate for the small percentage of students who simply cannot master the basic facts because that is part of their disability and they should be allowed to use calculators, in line with the National Council of Teachers of Mathematics (NCTM) guidelines. For those who can learn basic facts yet use calculators, the research is mixed on whether accommodations such as calculator usage increase the performance of these students (Tindal & Ketterlin-Geller, 2004). As students want to be independent at this age and research shows fostering self-directness enhances achievement (Montague, 2007), they respond well to support that allows them to take charge of their learning of these facts, in the following ways.

Data-Informed Instruction 6

To determine which students need support with basic facts, students can take the preassessment shown in Figure 4.1, and teachers can note when it is turned in. The timing should be discrete—for example, use a timer on a small computer screen—or it might heighten anxiety. Teachers should have the entire class do this, and note time needed on each. Then class norms can be used to determine which students perform these most slowly and so would need practice to increase their speed.

To differentiate which students know the facts, but are slow, from those who lack conceptual strategies for solving them, the last question asks them to explain strategies for solving various problems. Students can self-score these preassessments with blue ink ("all pencils away") and then create a plan for how they will learn the strategies and increase their speed (see Figure 4.2). Students should be given the opportunity to retake alternate versions of the test every 2 weeks before or after school or during a lab or free period. When they ask to set up an appointment to retake the quiz, they must bring a log of how and when they practiced (see Figure 4.3). Some teachers have difficulty getting students to make an effort to improve and retake the quiz every 2 weeks, so they mark down a student's homework grade.

Figure 4.1

Basic Facts

1.	9×8	$96 \div 12$	$17 - 9$	$3 + 8$
2.	$9 + 7$	7×8	$42 \div 6$	6×4
3.	$5 + 8$	$12 - 4$	6×7	$7 + 8$
4.	$3 + 6$	12×7	$7 + 4$	$12 - 5$
5.	$6 + 8$	$11 - 5$	$13 - 7$	$14 - 8$
6.	$4 + 7$	$15 - 8$	$16 - 9$	7×6
7.	$48 \div 6$	$21 \div 3$	3×6	8×6
8.	7×4	$14 - 8$	$8 + 4$	$14 - 9$

Explain how a person who can't recall a fact can solve:

6×7 $84 \div 12$

$8 + 7$ $17 - 9$

Figure 4.2

My Plan to Improve My Basic Calculations

Based on my preassessment, I'd like to improve:　　speed　　or　　accuracy (circle one).

The kinds of errors I made were:

_____

_____

_____

_____

_____

_____

_____

The problems I figured out most slowly or couldn't recall were:

$+$

$-$

$\times$

$\div$

My plan to improve is:

Resources:

Websites:

Distributed times I'll practice:

Figure 4.3

My Practice Log

Date	What I Did	Adult Signature
_____	_____	_____
_____	_____	_____
_____	_____	_____
_____	_____	_____
_____	_____	_____
_____	_____	_____
_____	_____	_____
_____	_____	_____
_____	_____	_____
_____	_____	_____

My Graph (Goal: Number per minute)

5

4

3

2

1

(Min)

Dates ___ ___ ___ ___ ___ ___ ___ ___ ___ ___

Knows Facts but Slow Recall—Use Speeded Retrieval Strategies

For students like Beverly who know their facts but recall them slowly, they can use varied practice options such as using timers as they take timed fact tests. They can chart their time and accuracy on graphs (refer to Figure 4.3) and set goals for each successive practice. In addition, they can use cover, copy, compare types of strategies in which they do the following:

1. Copy a fact reading it aloud.

2. Cover it up.

3. Write it from memory.

4. Compare it to the original problem (adapted from Stading, Williams, & McLaughlin, 1996).

Teachers can have students who need to strengthen these skills work in pairs quizzing each other or have students bring in signed evidence that they worked on these at home. In addition, students can also use motivating practices such as games at www.multiplication.com, particularly "The Magician," or http://www.tomsnyder.com/fasttmath/index.html. The Magician gives a certificate when students master a certain number of problems in a given time, and fast-t charts progress, but it is a pay site. FASTT tracks students usage and provides progress monitoring quizzes every set times of practices, such as every hour. Many more sites exist, as typing "multiplication games" into a search engine shows. When selecting websites (or having students select them), keep the following in mind:

Factors to Consider in Selecting Online Practice

- Does the game have a quick pace? (time on task)
- How many problems are solved per minute?
- Is it a timed practice?
- Does the game offer immediate feedback and corrections?
- Does the game chart progress?
- Is there a competitive element, that is, a high scorer's list?
- Can it be set up so only unknown facts are practiced?

One site has students navigate through a cave to find facts to practice. Most time is spent on navigating and little on practicing facts. Charting progress and moving up on high scorer lists can be super engaging and motivating, as on www.iknowthat.com. The website www.coolmath-games.com can be set up so students practice only those facts that they need to learn, as does FASTT. Other websites such as www.algebrahelp.com and www.mathscore.com provide personalized feedback and differentiated tips on how to improve.

Needs Conceptual Understanding of Basic Facts

In addition to drill, those students like Steven who have not mastered their basic facts because of conceptual problems benefit from learning strategies for figuring out the answers. It is essential that students practice responding correctly when practicing these facts so that if they do not know the correct responses, they can best learn them using strategies described below. In fact, research has found that when both drill and the kind of strategy instruction described in this section are integrated, the two approaches result in the greatest gains and transfer (Woodward, 2006), and so this makes the argument that both should be taught to all students.

Strategy instruction enables students to understand the relationships between basic facts so that they can use these to better understand them and remember them more efficiently. Students decompose numbers in the following ways. For example, if a student knows $3 \times 7 = 21$, then 6×7 can be decomposed and figured out by doubling 21 to get 42. Or if they know $6 + 6$, they can use this to solve $6 + 7$. The following are excellent resources for reinforcing such a strategic approach to learning basic facts:

- Dale Seymour's *Mental Math* series (addition and subtraction)
- Sopris West's *Fact Fluency and More!* (addition and subtraction)
- http://www.mathscore.com (addition, subtraction, multiplication, and division)

Students should monitor their own progress with weekly quizzes and should be sure to graph their progress (refer to Figure 4 3) so they can monitor the effectiveness of the approaches they are using. Fuchs and Fuchs (1986) have found that such progress monitoring is highly effective, particularly when graphed and used with data-based decision rules such as: If after seven attempts, students' graphed scores are not increasing, encourage them to practice with an alternative strategy, or in a more distributed way (over time, rather than all at once). Possible sequences for teaching these calculation strategies are shown in Figure 4.4.

To further deepen students' understandings of basic facts, mathematical representations can be used to model concepts. As an example, Fosnot and Dolk (2001) demonstrate how arrays of numbers can be used to help students construct understandings of basic facts through seeing pictorial number arrays, a research-based practice recommended by The What Works Clearing House's Math Practice Guide (Gersten et al., 2009). In this approach, students see how four rows of six can transform into an arrangement of three rows of eight, with the number of chips or dots representing the total of 24 remaining constant.

Explicit and Systematic Instruction

Teaching basic skills can be introduced in a constructivist, discovery-oriented approach, but some students will require explicit and systematic instruction. These need not be opposing approaches. The teachers in the

Figure 4.4

Basic Facts Calculation Strategies

Addition Facts

I have mastered:

Count on (Use when adding 1 or 2. Start with larger number, then count up 1 or 2)   _____

Doubles and Neighbors (i.e., 4 + 4, so 4 + 5)

Neighbors (8 + 7 ≈ double 7 plus 1 more)   _____

Five-Bars (5 + 1; 5 + 7 ≈ 5 + 5 + 2)   _____

Ten-Frames (2 + 8; 4 + 6; 7 + 3)

Nearly 10: All 9 facts (5 + 4, 7 + 2) and 11 facts (3 + 8; 4 + 7)   _____

Decomposing numbers—10 facts with 8 or 9   _____

8 + 6 = (decompose 6 into 2 + 4) 8 + 2 which is 10, then +4, so a total of 14

Remaining 8 facts: 8 + 4, 6 + 8   _____

Multiplication Facts

I have mastered:

0, 1, 10, 11—Instant patterns   _____

2, 5—Double the number or count by 5s   _____

Doubles (2 × 2, 3 × 3 . . .)   _____

Double the doubles: 3 × 7 = 21; so 6 × 7—double 21 is 42   _____

The 9-times quickie (think of 10 fact, subtract a 9)   _____

Use a related fact, i.e., add one more (6 × 8 + 8 = 7 × 8)   _____

6s—Think-of-5 fact, add one more (5 × 8 + 8 = 6 × 8)   _____

3s—Think of 2, add one more   _____

focus groups I led were deeply committed to a constructivist, discovery-oriented approach, yet when students needed additional supports, they had a wide array of explicit and systematic options to use to offer this, often as a backup, which included providing written models of proficient problem solving, encouraging students to verbalize thought processes, having students engage in guided practice with corrective feedback offered, and frequent cumulative review, all of which are strongly supported by research according to The What Works Clearing House's Middle School Math Practice Guide (Gersten et al., 2009).

DIFFERENTIATING FOR CONCEPTUAL UNDERSTANDING

Elizabeth shrank back when she heard that the next unit would be on geometry. She knows her learning style well, and she knows that she has difficulty interpreting visual images. When her teacher had recently tried to explain fractions through visual images, she noticed that Elizabeth actually looked away. Elizabeth is a cooperative student and eager to learn, but it was an epiphany for them both when they realized that she did this because she just cannot make sense of images. Elizabeth has a mild nonverbal learning disability, which often means that she struggles with making sense of nonverbal images, and she prefers to learn through words.

Teddy usually performs well on math tasks, though not extraordinarily well. However, on a recent probability task, he had real difficulty understanding the idea of independent events. His teacher drew a diagram for him, but he still did not seem to get the concept. Teddy has no diagnosed disability; he just often requires more time, exposures, and practice to master certain conceptual understandings.

Students who struggle with conceptual understanding can pose some of the toughest challenges for teachers. Often teachers feel most of the class is ready to move on but recognize some need more time. The following approaches are designed to be used as homework or tiers built into full class lessons so the whole class is not held up while a few students get extra help with a concept. It is recommended that teachers focus on developing and solidifying conceptual understandings before procedures, as recommended in NCTM's (2000) Learning Principle that cautions against teaching procedures without fully addressing conceptual understanding as well. A continued emphasis on solidifying conceptual understandings is prominent in the new core standards for mathematics as well (http://www.corestandards.org).

Clarify a Concept and Assess It

Before attempting to use a more intensive strategy to help strengthen a student's grasp of a concept, teachers should ensure they themselves have a clear sense of the specifics of the concept that they would like to develop as well as precisely where the student falls on a continuum of understanding the concept. Teachers can ask themselves questions such as:

- What are the specifics of the concept I want the student to grasp?
- What is already grasped?
- What else can I try to develop it?

To determine what the student already does understand, the teacher can sit with the student and ask him or her to verbalize their thought processes or explain their thinking, with prompts such as, "Tell me all you do understand." However, teachers often don't have the luxury of this time, and so they can have students fill in a form such as Figure 4.5. Often just having students complete this form, which requires them to focus on what they do know, crystallizes their questions. After the teacher has these data, alternative approaches for clarifying the concept can be chosen from the following list of strategies. Research supporting each is given in the following sections:

- Manipulatives: Concrete-representational-abstract learning sequence (CRA)
- Graphic organizers
- Diagramming
- Coresearching alternative explanations

These strategies are described in more detail in the following sections.

Manipulatives: Concrete-Representational-Abstract Learning Sequence

Students can also gain conceptual understandings through working with manipulatives, though teachers need to tread cautiously to ensure these are novel, small, and not perceived as childish (though some teachers disagree that manipulatives would be perceived this way). If many students need this support, manipulatives can be used with the entire class regularly and approached with a mature attitude. Otherwise, a manipulative center can be set up in one area of the classroom, and students who need that practice can spend time there. ❼ In this way, a lesson can be easily differentiated. (See Chapter 6 for more on using centers to tier instruction.)

Differentiation of Student Work **7**

Research has found certain manipulatives used in a CRA learning sequence (CRA—concrete objects, representational or pictorial, then abstract or written symbols) uplifts algebra achievement (Witzel, 2005; Witzel, Mercer, & Miller, 2003). For a resource on this approach, see Riccomini and Witzel (2010a). Among the manipulatives available for middle school content that I and teachers in the focus groups I ran have found helpful are the following:

- Algebra tiles (linear and quadratic equation solving)
- Didax Geofix (nets)
- Models of shapes (surface area and volume)
- Soft 1 cm squares (available from (http://www.etacuisenaire.com)

For example, in a unit on exponents, manipulatives can be used to teach a concept through a tiered lesson. By having students build multiplicative growth models of 4 × 3 with small cubes and exponential growth models of 4^3, they can actually see the striking difference in

Figure 4.5

Concept Questions

A concept we are learning is:

_____

_____

_____

A diagram for understanding this is:

The parts I understand are:

_____

_____

_____

The questions I have are:

_____

_____

_____

how quickly the models grow in contrast to each other. This lesson can be instantly and easily differentiated in that students who immediately show that they already know exponents can move on to challenging activities, such as researching and writing an explanation for why a number raised to the power of zero is one. Again, these manipulatives should differ from those used in elementary school or they may be rejected as immature by middle school students. It is important to keep in mind that some students can gain abstract understandings without needing the concrete instructional phase and so they should be allowed to skip ahead.

As noted earlier, if only very few students need manipulatives, they should be offered as a station in a learning center, rather than a full class activity. After building models, students should then sketch diagrams of these kinds of models to move through the representational phase of this learning sequence. Finally, they can work with only the number symbols on paper. In general, when using manipulatives, researchers have found three exposures to manipulatives followed by three exposures to representations has ensured that many students with mathematics disabilities understand the concept (Miller & Hudson, 2007).

Graphic Organizers

Another key way to accommodate diverse learners that can be easily used at any time and during any unit of study is graphic organizers. Students who can grasp information when presented in a compact way with relationships among the pieces of information expressed symbolically benefit from graphic organizers. These can be presented in varied formats to help different kinds of learners all make sense of information. Excellent graphic organizers that have actually been tested and research has found to be effective are available at www.graphicorganizers.com. Note the

Polynomials		
Monomial (one term)	Binomial (polynomial of two terms)	Trinomial (polynomial of three terms)
5	$5a + 5b$	$5a + 6c + 12d$
X	$10h + 10i$	$x^2 + 2 \times 2 + 4 \times 3 + x$
$5b$	$10 + 12i$	$4 \times 2 + 3 \times 2 + 6x$ (nonexample)
$\dfrac{1}{5}$	$7y - 2x$	$3 + 4x + x^2$
$\dfrac{10}{2}$	$3x - 4x$ (nonexample)	

sample graphic organizer that shows how monomials, binomials, and trinomials fall under the umbrella category of polynomials.

Research has found that using graphic organizers results in improved performance in areas such as solving linear equations (Ives, 2007). Lessons can be differentiated in that some students can be asked to create graphic organizers on their own, while others are given support for creating them with models or templates, such as that in Figure 4.6.

Diagramming

Most textbooks recommend students make diagrams but give little direct instruction for how to do so. With diagrams, students learn how to map relationships within common word problems visually into diagrams. Since students with learning needs often have difficulty understanding visual and numerical relationships, diagramming may be one of the most important and potentially widely used strategies worth teaching. Diagramming can enable students to understand concepts or problems through designing solution plans that keep track of their thinking while solving word problems (Marshall, 1995). As the brain is hard wired to create and use schemas that can be represented in diagrams, this facilitates how students naturally organize their interpretation and solution for word problems.

Research has found that using schematic images is positively related to success in mathematical problem-solving, whereas the use of pictorial images (irrelevant to the math, e.g., coloring petals on flowers along a road in a distance problem) is negatively related to success (Van Garderen, 2006). Schematic representations were used to *correctly* solve problems most of the time, whereas pictorial representations were used most of the time for *incorrect* solutions. Pictorial representations include drawings that focus on irrelevant aspects of the problem while schematic images use codes or symbols to show relationships.

Students should use the most time-efficient strategies for drawing diagrams. They should be told that diagrams should not be realistic pictures, but just quick symbols or codes to show relationships between mathematical models. Students could even practice drawing inefficient diagrams (with trees and leaves along a road between two boys' homes) and then more efficient ones like those in Figure 4.7.

A diagram can be used as a tool to show initial understanding of a problem, to show how it tracks what is happening in the problem, and to justify the solution (Van Gardener, 2006). When using it to track thinking, marks such as arrows that show flow should be outside the diagram to avoid confusion. Teachers should repeatedly emphasize that diagrams are not products, but just tools to model thinking. Furthermore, some diagrams that model relationships have been found to be more effective than those that are set up in a way that less clearly

Figure 4.6

Designing a Graphic Organizer

A concept we are learning now is:

Different categories of this concept are:

Differences among the pieces of the categories are:

List each category in the box.

List distinguishing factors below.

Figure 4.7

Diagram Types

The following are four categories of diagram types:

1. Networks or line diagrams

Peter and Tom live 1,000 feet apart. Tom walks twice as fast as Peter. If they planned to meet and leave at the same time, how many feet will each walk?

This type works best for problems that can be presented in a line.

2. Matrices or tables

3. Tree diagram

Sprinkle	Caramel	Fruit
^	^	^
Vanilla or Chocolate	Vanilla or Chocolate	Vanilla or Chocolate

4. Part to whole

Near a pond, there were 22 sets of footprints from each animal. The two types of animals were ducks and rabbits. How many were there of each type?

Sources: Van Gardener, 2006; Xin, 2007.

models relationships between quantities; an example of this is ******—ooo to show a decrease by a factor of 2 (Xin, Jitendra, & Deatline-Buchman, 2005).

Xin and Jitendra (2006) offer research validated strategies for teaching students to diagram such rate and ratio in proportion problems. A full curriculum for teaching this strategy is available from Pro Ed (Jitendra, 2007).

Figure 4.8

Creating My Own Diagram

My diagram:

_____

_____

_____

_____

_____

This diagram shows:

_____

_____

_____

_____

_____

Diagram Checklists

1. Does it show all relevant parts of the math problem? (not necessarily everything)

2. Does it show how these parts are related? (how they belong together)

3. Does it lead into a solution?

4. Is there any extra information or details that can be deleted?

5. Did I draw it as quickly but accurately as possible? (does not need to be realistic)

6. Did I use codes? (teacher to demonstrate)

7. Can I show how I track my understanding of the problem with it?

8. Can I use it to explain how I justify my solution?

Students should first determine whether the given word problem fits into the structure of the "vary" type of problem diagram. "Vary" problems are those in which two amounts vary in relation to one another. These are common types of problems that students encounter in middle school such as ratio, rates and proportion, making this a useful strategy to learn.

In addition, Xin and Jitendra (2006) recommend that when readiness levels show a need, teachers can begin by presenting all available information to students at first so that there is nothing to solve for while the process is being introduced and modeled. Students merely gain practice in how to set up the diagrams, as in the following example:

A car travels 25 miles on a gallon of gas. It can travel 75 miles on 3 gallons of gas. (Jitendra, 2002)

After students are comfortable with diagramming, then problems with missing information can be diagrammed.

Coresearching Alternative Explanations

When students are having difficulty mastering a topic, teachers and students should explore multiple explanations in alternative textbooks or on the Internet. *Transitional Mathematics Program* (Woodward & Stroh, 2004) published by Sopris West is an alternative text with clear direct instruction and explanations, designed for students who struggle.

As an example of research on a topic, students might be invited to find three definitions of what a transversal is and how this can be used to calculate angle measures in parallel lines crossed by a transversal. The different websites might offer varied verbal descriptions, visuals, and examples. Using a guide like Figure 4.9, students could then select which  they prefer and explain why. To structure this type of task, teachers can create hotlists or webquests of diverse and high-quality websites that students can access to find such comparisons, such as www.kn.sbc.com/wired/fil/pages/listallthinli.html.

This site presents links to varied geometry Web pages. Additional good sites include:

http://www.eduplace.com/kids/hmm (concept review, math glossary, games)

http://www.sadlier-oxford.com/math (concept review, math minutes)

As a word of caution, be sure to check all links and ensure they are active before using an existing hotlist. Also, if teachers do not have sufficient Internet access for the entire class to be online at once, students can work in groups or could use alternative texts to do similar activities as one group uses the Internet. Free sample math texts are often available from most publishers.

Figure 4.9

Alternative Sources Project

Concept I explored:

_____

_____

_____

_____

Sources I used:

_____

_____

_____

Summary of explanations:

_____

_____

_____

The best one was_____ because

_____

_____

_____

Teach Students Time Management

One of the realities of having a learning challenge is that schoolwork inevitably takes more time, even when students are using top notch learning strategies. Once students grasp a concept, it is not *learned.* To hang on to it, they must do distributed practice until it is internalized. How much practice varies and so needs to be differentiated, as I have found over-drill once a concept is mastered can actually decrease learning. Some students will simply require more time, particularly when teachers give students the option to work on their homework in class while helping students who need extra help. The students who receive the extra help in class will not get the time to work on their homework. If available, teachers can refer these students to a counselor or another specialist who can help them with time management. Such students could be asked to fill out a time management form. As time management is a great topic for all students, the form could be offered to all. To avoid losing class teaching time, it could be given as a homework assignment. To strengthen the value that students get from it, they could be asked to work on it with an adult.

DIFFERENTIATING PROCEDURAL SUPPORT

Leo's eyes light up whenever he is given a challenging math problem that he can really sink his teeth into and think about deeply. However, Leo becomes frustrated whenever he needs to perform basic mathematical procedural calculations such as long division or multiplying decimals because he has long-term memory difficulties that cause him to forget the simple steps needed to perform these and so he constantly makes accidental miscalculations. Nevertheless, he enjoys toying with mathematical problems that intrigue him.

Jason, on the other hand, has a solid long-term memory of how to perform these kinds of calculations because he has over practiced them over the years. However, Jason struggles with attentional and working memory problems that cause him to forget steps or do steps out of order when he is working on learning new algorithms such as how to solve linear equations. When calculating, he needs support with organizing how to approach solving a problem, then with monitoring his thinking as he carries out the steps.

This section addresses difficulties students have with following procedures: taking the right steps in the right order to perform calculations, after conceptual understandings have been built and students merely need support with recalling steps, or the order of steps. First, strategies are recommended for students like Leo who need backfilling; practicing basic calculations such as long division or multiplying fractions and decimals, skills needed for middle school math. Next, general and content-based strategies are presented for students like Jason who have difficulty with mastering procedures, even after understanding concepts behind them. Again, as a caveat—some students will have inordinate difficulty mastering basic facts because of the nature of their disability. Others will be so put off by the practice that teachers need to weigh how important it is to teach these against potentially fostering a dislike of mathematics globally because these have been over-taught. I have attempted to cite the most motivating and enjoyable ways to learn these. However, if a student is just not making progress and is not receiving the kind of innate satisfaction that comes from mastering these, then placing too much emphasis on them needs to be reconsidered and options such as calculator use explored.

As students self-score their basic fact preassessments (refer to Figure 4.1), they should also take and self-score the basic calculations preassessment (see Figure 4.10). Then in Figure 4.11, they are given an array of options for how they can take steps to improve. ❹ It is important they keep track of these efforts, graph improvements on each subsequent retaking of the preassessment, and determine if their chosen strategy is helping them improve. Teachers should tread cautiously in recommending strategies, or students might groan and complain at strategies such as "checklists," feeling that it is being imposed rather than embrace it as valuable. Students are more likely to appreciate the value of strategies when they self-direct which they choose and how they use them.

Student Self-Direction **4**

Figure 4.10

Basic Calculations Preassessment

$2\frac{1}{3} + 4\frac{5}{8}$ $6\frac{1}{5} \div 1\frac{2}{3}$

$482.01 \div 9.6$ 5.82×63.09

$\frac{3}{8} \times 4\frac{1}{4}$ $33.6 \div 9.807$

$2\frac{1}{5} - 1\frac{4}{7}$ $99 - 3.08$

$3 \div 8$ $3.6 \div 0.006$

Backfilling Basic Calculations

Students like Leo show up with gaps in their ability to perform basic calculations. Basic calculations are distinguished from basic skills in that calculations involve longer procedures (long division) in contrast to a simple fact $(7 + 8)$. As noted earlier, teachers can give a brief pretest to the entire class in the beginning of the year to find which students need to strengthen their ability to perform basic calculations (refer to Figure 4.10). Students who cannot complete all the calculations accurately within a reasonable timeframe can be expected to design a practice plan (refer to Figure 4.11) and to retake the test every 2–4 weeks until they are able to pass it. Before taking it, they should submit the same practice log recommended in the basic facts section (see refer to Figure 4.3) with a graph of improvements. Ideally, they should be able to make their own, or at least research and find ones that appeal to them on the Internet. For example, the following is a sample mnemonic to help students recall the steps of long division:

Figure 4.11

My Practice Plan for Basic Calculations

My preassessment shows I need to practice:

Circle each:

  Addition of fractions/decimals

  Subtraction of fractions/decimals

  Multiplication of fractions/decimals

  Division of fractions/decimals

List where I had difficulty (which step) for each:

_____

_____

_____

_____

_____

_____

_____

My plan for practicing this is (be specific—list websites/resources):

_____

_____

_____

_____

_____

_____

DMSB—Divide Multiply Subtract Bring Down
Dracula must suck blood.

A major key with such mnemonics is that they provide cues and help students organize themselves, two facets of successful instruction with students with learning challenges, according to the research (Swanson & Deshler, 2003). Again, it should be stressed that these tricks should only be used with students who fully understand the concept. More of this type exists, including whole rap songs.

Distributed Practice

Distributed (spread out over time) rather than massed (done all at once) practice should be recommended. Students can do distributed practice at many websites, and with self-correcting worksheet puzzles such as Math With Pizzazz (Marcy & Marcy, 1989). These puzzles have students solve problems, then use the answers to solve a puzzle. If a wrong answer is calculated, the answer will not appear in the puzzle and the student will get instant feedback that the answer needs to be reworked.

Checklists

Checklists are an effective way to help students understand and mentally organize procedural routines that can be used in many versatile ways. Research has found that even in isolation, when used alone rather than as part of a comprehensive strategy, checklists can significantly support low achieving, bringing their performance level close to their peers and that all students reporting enjoying using them (Zrebiec Uberti, Mastropieri, & Scruggs, 2004).

Checklists provide an instant tier in a lesson plan. When teaching the area of triangles, for example, teachers can have some students move on to challenge problems in class, while giving students who show they are having difficulty with recalling the necessary steps scaffolded support in creating step checklists (see Figure 4.12). See also the example of a student-created checklist that was designed to address the specific kinds of errors this student made most frequently in finding the area of a triangle. Students should be expected to fade using this scaffold as they become comfortable with the needed steps.

Sample Student-Created Checklist

☐ Did I identify the type of triangle? If it is not a right triangle, do I know what to do?
☐ Did I recall the formula for the triangle? Did I divide by 2 (or multiply by $\frac{1}{2}$)? If not, where can I find the formula?
☐ Did I identify base and height?
☐ Did I identify a height that is perpendicular to the base?
☐ Did I diagram it? (Can I see this in relation to a square/rectangle?)
☐ Did I label it?
☐ Can I justify the reasonableness of my response?

Figure 4.12

Making a Checklist of Procedural Steps

List all steps I need to do (number them and read them to someone who can do the procedure):

_____

_____

_____

_____

_____

_____

_____

Write the steps as questions to ask yourself to self-direct you through the process.

_____

_____

_____

_____

_____

_____

_____

_____

When/How will you practice these?

_____

_____

_____

Heuristics—Specific Strategies for Remembering a Sequence of Steps

In addition to checklists, students can be helped to design and use strategies for remembering sequences of steps needed for procedures through heuristics. Recent research has found that among those strategies that significantly uplift achievement among students with learning disabilities in mathematics, those that apply heuristics are by far the most powerful (Gersten, Chard, Jayanthi, Baker, Morphy, & Flojo, 2009). Students with some learning needs have difficulty with monitoring and directing their thinking while they engage in solving math problems (Montague, 2007), particularly following procedural steps. The following strategies, which are examples of heuristics, can be offered to all students, to assist them with following procedural steps if checklists are not enough support.

Look-Ask-Pick

Look-Ask-Pick (LAP) is an example of a procedural strategy that is somewhat of a heuristic, in that it is used to teach students the specific steps for solving one type of math problem. LAP was developed and validated by Test and Ellis (2005) to help students understand the necessary steps for adding and subtracting fractions.

LAP: Adding and Subtracting Fractions

Look at the denominators $(\frac{1}{2} + \frac{1}{3})$

Ask yourself the questions: Are they the *same*/Will the smaller denominator divide into the larger denominator an even number of times? (No.)

Pick your fraction type. (They fit into sixths.)

The steps for teaching LAP include:

- ☐ Teacher modeling of the strategy.
- ☐ Guided practice of the steps with the teacher and students restating the steps.
- ☐ Individual practice of the strategy steps.
- ☐ Pair practice using games and flash cards to recall the strategy steps and types of fractions.

Source: Test & Ellis, 2005.

A strategy like this can be posted in the classroom or placed on small laminated cards and given to students to hold at their desks. After addressing any prerequisite skill gaps and gaining buy-in from students through discussing when and how it will be useful to them, the teacher can model the strategy with a think-aloud and ensure students learn it through activities such as reciting or writing each step before entering or leaving the classroom.

Students can initially use checklists they have developed to ask themselves whether they have correctly carried out each step as a means of evaluating how they implemented the strategy. These can then be faded. As students continue to practice LAP, they too can draft think-alouds (based on their checklist) so that the teacher can observe how each step is applied and offer feedback. Having students write think-alouds is also important so that they practice instructing themselves because this maximizes the potential that students will internalize the strategy and use it when not directly reminded to do so.

All students may not need to learn this strategy and so they won't need to complete the self-directed learning plan. Instead, they can work on independent projects, self-correcting materials (exercises with answers available), or other types of activities. To reinforce instruction, students could also then teach these types of strategies to the larger class. Offering them to the larger class can also remove any stigma that these students might feel when they see their peers choose to use them as well.

Parentheses, Exponents, Multiplication and Division, and Addition and Subtraction

Another sample heuristic, also called a mnemonic, for recalling the order of steps needed when performing multiple operations is PEMDAS, which stands for Parentheses, Exponents, Multiplication and Division, and Addition and Subtraction. When solving multiple-step computation problems, PEMDAS (or Please Excuse My Dear Aunt Sally) tells you the ranks of the operations: Parentheses outrank exponents, which outrank multiplication and division (but multiplication and division are at the *same* rank), and these two outrank addition and subtraction (which again are together on the bottom rank). The meaning of why PEMDAS works can be conveyed through having students solve word problems such as Jonah receives $25 from Sefu and $5 from each one of his three other friends. Students will immediately see that if they solve $25 + $5 × 3 without using PEMDAS, they will not be able to justify the reasonableness of the solution (see Sanjay, 2002, for a fuller explanation).

Read-Identify-Diagram-Evaluate

An additional heuristic students can use to carry out a more generic sequence of procedures that can be applied to variety of types of problems (such as any type of word problem) is the following modification of RIDE (Read Identify Diagram Evaluate),which was developed by Mercer and Mercer (1993). This strategy can be used to teach students how to approach solving a word problem. For students who require more support, a single step of RIDE, such as diagram relationships, can be expanded to include substeps as needed. This strategy can be taught in the same way as described for LAP.

RIDE

- **R**ead problem carefully, slowly and entirely.
- **I**dentify relevant information and highlight it.
- **D**iagram relationships in a way that leads to a solution.

  Create simple symbols for each piece of critical information.

- **E**valuate your answer with computation and justify its reasonableness.

Source: Mercer & Mercer, 1993.

To gain buy-in to any strategy, students can complete the debriefing sheet shown in Figure 4.13.

Designing Strategies

Students can be encouraged to design their own strategies and to tailor those aspects of the routines that they find most helpful to meet their own individual needs. Teachers often make the mistake of moving on too quickly and teaching a new strategy before the first is fully internalized. As a rule of thumb, my experience has shown that students should learn no more than two to three strategies per year in their first years of learning these.

A few guidelines are cited in Ellis and Lenz (1996), who identified a number of critical features for creating successful mnemonics for these kinds of strategies. These have been summarized in Hudson and Miller (2006), who write that the strategy should contain steps that lead to the problem solution, the steps should be generalizable to other similar problems, each step in the strategy should begin with an action word, and each step should be as brief as possible. The first letter of each action word for each step should be a mnemonic, as in the example RIDE.

Essentially, according to Ellis and Lenz (1996), the steps should use research-validated principles of learning such as setting goals, activating background knowledge, or self-monitoring one's own work. They should not be just a loose collection of suggestions for separate tasks. They should use the minimal number of steps needed and be organized in the most efficient and comprehensive way. Each step must be essential, not "Open your book." Steps need to be thorough, and the entire process broken down fully. Although this may seem inefficient, adults often forget all the small substeps we had to take when initially learning a procedure. Ellis and Lenz (1996) present a valuable checklist that can be used to evaluate the potential effectiveness of any strategy.

In the next chapter, strategies suited for differentiating for math talented students are presented.

Figure 4.13

Strategy Debriefing Sheet

The strategy I used was:

_____

_____

_____

_____

I used it in the following way:

_____

_____

_____

_____

It helped me improve by:

_____

_____

_____

_____

5

Challenging Students Who Are High Achieving

Students who are regularly high achieving in mathematics often crave intellectual stimulation. Finding or designing just the right level of challenge that is neither too easy, nor beyond their grasp can be challenging for teachers. These students often react emotionally when they are bored with easy work, or they disengage when work is too much of a reach. When the work is right at their challenge level, they exhibit an almost perceptible sense of enjoyment in their engagement. Their body language or comments offer valuable feedback that teachers can use to make instructional changes and inform future planning decisions. Essentially, students' responses to the work they are given provide valuable guidance, which is important to use as a gauge since less empirical research on teaching this population exists than for others. The research that does exist (Tieso, 2005) suggests that two broad factors should be kept in mind when planning for the students: exemptions and higher order thinking.

One caveat to bear in mind that I often hear from practitioners that is true for this chapter, as well as for the previous chapter, is that the strategies mentioned in both of these chapters are often good for all students.

EXEMPTIONS BASED ON PRIOR KNOWLEDGE OR PACE OF LEARNING

Two major reasons exist as to why students should be allowed to be exempt from completing all of the regular work assigned to the entire class. First, when formative assessments reveal a student has already mastered certain information, then that student should be exempt from having to complete some or all of the practice material. Second, although some students may not have been exposed to certain math content before and so will not recognize it on preassessments, they learn at an accelerated pace. They master new material far more quickly than do their peers and require fewer repetitions of practice problems to achieve this. Therefore, they should also be exempt from regular amounts of practice.

Yet, meeting the needs of the second group requires greater flexibility on the part of the teacher because it requires shifting gears, often mid-lesson, when it becomes apparent that some have mastered the topic and so are ready to move ahead more quickly than others. Ideally, teachers will have predicted this and will have alternate activities prepared. However, at times this can happen unexpectedly. For that reason it can be helpful to keep emergency spare folder of challenges on hand to be used rarely. These challenges should never be extra work but should instead *replace* work that is unnecessary. When students clearly master a concept after doing half the required practice, they can do the challenges in place of the unnecessary practice. Challenges should always be viewed as replacements and not as extra work.

Dale Seymour publishes excellent mathematical challenge materials that can be used for this purpose. The journal *Mathematics Teaching in the Middle School* also often publishes excellent challenges that can be copied and saved. In addition, these students may participate in math competitions, and so making challenge problems from resources such as "Math Counts" or "Math Olympiads" available to them can be helpful as well. However, programs for math talented students are often criticized for merely offering such types of ancillary enrichment. More substantial enrichment with a scope and sequence that is tied more closely to the curricular topic being taught to the full class is preferable and will be described later in this chapter. The above suggestions are merely for those unanticipated times when students appear disengaged while having to wait for peers to master material that they have already mastered.

Strategies for Instant Enrichment

As mentioned, teachers can keep folders with enriching activities on hand for unexpected times when some students are ready to move on and others are not. In addition, and more strongly recommended, teachers can offer instant enrichment through asking students who have completed their work early the following kinds of questions related to the current work:

- Can you solve this problem in another way?
- Design and explain an alternative new algorithm for solving this problem.
- Describe several ways to solve this, then defend which is the most efficient and why.

These types of immediate extensions can be posted in a classroom. When students announce, "I'm done," teachers can merely point to these options so that the classroom culture shifts from students looking to the teacher for enrichment to students knowing where and how they can find it for themselves.

Curriculum Compacting

One strategy for exempting students from regular practice is called curriculum compacting (Winebrenner, 2001). In this strategy, the assignment is literally compacted. Based on preassessments, teachers can determine in advance to allow some students to only complete alternate problems or just the final problems on a page, as these usually provide practice but are also often the most difficult problems as well. It is a constant judgment call to determine the exact amount of practice each student requires, because these students do require some practice, just not as much as their peers. The amount they need differs, as students who are math talented are a heterogeneous group. Teachers need to beware that students can sometimes appear to understand the concept, yet may not have mastered it until they receive some amount of drill. Alternatively, when teachers realize mid-lesson that some students should move more quickly, they can compact *on the fly* and allow students to do fewer problems. From experience, it is wise to make notes on students' papers and in one's grade book when doing this, because it can be easy to forget which students were told to do what.

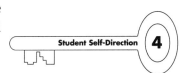

Codesigned Learning Contracts

When preassessments reveal that a student has already mastered the majority of a new unit, it may sometimes be helpful to design learning contracts with that student (see Figure 5.1). These work well with students who are exceptionally well directed. Students can complete these at home, after taking a preassessment. They can then come in and see the teacher before or after school, or at another convenient time set to discuss the plan. The teacher may attach a list of challenges and projects that coordinate with the unit topic for the student to reference when proposing alternative work to do.

Figure 5.1

Math Learning Contract

Summary of what the preassessment shows I have mastered:

_____

_____

_____

_____

_____

I still need to learn:

_____

_____

_____

_____

_____

My plan for learning this is:

_____

_____

_____

_____

_____

In place of the work that I have already mastered, I will:

Parallel-Related Curriculum

Another option for students who have already mastered unit concepts is for them to work on a parallel, related curricular topic during the unit. This option works better for students who benefit from more structure. On the preassessment, items from this parallel curriculum can also be assessed to ensure that students don't already know the parallel curricular topic as well. For example, the following absolute value questions were placed at the end of integers preassessment. Several of the students who performed well on the preassessment missed these questions, so they worked on these types of problems in place of the regular class material that their preassessments had shown they had already mastered (see Figure 5.2).

Differentiation of Student Work 7

Figure 5.2

Integers Parallel Curriculum

Determine whether each statement is true.

Justify the reasonableness of your opinion for each.

1. If $x < 0$ and $y > 0$, then $x - y > 0$
2. If $x > 0$ and $y > 0$, then $x + y < 0$
3. If $x < 0$ and $y < 0$, then $x - y > 0$
4. If $x < 0$ and $y < 0$, then $x + y > 0$
5. If $x < y$, then $x - y > 0$
6. If $x > y$, then $x - y > 0$
7. If $x > 0$ and $y < 0$, then $x - y > 0$
8. If $x < 0$ and $y < 0$, and $x - y > 0$, then $|x + y| > 0$
9. If $x < 0$, then $-(-x)$ is positive
10. If x and y are negative integers, then $x + y$ is negative
11. If x and y are positive integers, then $|x + y| = |x| + |y|$
12. If x and y are integers, and $x + 2 > y + 2$, then $|x| > |y|$
13. If x and y are integers and $5 - x < 5 - y$, then $|x| < |y|$
14. If $(x) + (-y) =$ a positive integer, then $|x| > |y|$

OPPORTUNITIES FOR HIGHER ORDER MATH

Students who complete work early because preassessments show they already know the material or because they master it more quickly than their peers should use their freed up time to engage in higher order math challenges that are not viewed as extra work, but as replacement or enrichment work. Various enrichment options have been described in prior chapters. Yet, some students need more than these types of enrichment. They learn in qualitatively different ways from their peers. They do not just need harder or more advanced work. They need opportunities to engage in higher order thinking. Although each child is unique, certain patterns or common traits exist that these students share. These patterns or traits can be helpful to bear in mind when planning for these students.

Researchers of mathematically gifted middle school students have proposed various models for categorizing how these students think mathematically. For example, Sak (2009) has proposed that three major categories of gifted mathematical minds exist: knowledge expert, creative, and analytical. The knowledge expert shows an extraordinary ability for memory recall and routine problem-solving. The creative mind excels at intuition/induction and using novel ways to produce new knowledge. Finally, the analytical mind excels at logical deduction/proof and reproducing knowledge.

This framework can be helpful in guiding the kind of enrichment that will best suit the type of mathematical strengths that different students show. For example, knowledge experts would probably thrive from being given opportunities to tackle accelerated math challenges. Creatively minded students might enjoy an opportunity to design a new algorithm. Alternatively, if a student shows a strength in one area, the teacher might want to give the child an opportunity to develop strengths in other areas.

Another, less analytical, model for understanding students who are high achieving in mathematics is to consider the abilities that are common to students who have been identified as math talented or gifted (Greenes, 1981). These include the following:

- Spontaneous formation of problems
- Flexibility in handling data
- Fluency of ideas
- Data organization abilities
- Originality of interpretation
- Ability to transfer ideas
- Ability to generalize

Carol Tieso's (2005) research on math talented students provides concrete examples of exactly how higher order thinking skills can be taught. In this research, students taught in small homogenous groups, with repetitive and unchallenging material replaced with the following kinds of real-life complex dilemmas, far outperformed ability-matched peers who were taught in the full class with the regular curriculum. Specifically, during a unit on data analysis, this study used a newspaper article that revealed how baseball statistics can be manipulated to further certain private agendas. This idea, of relating a unit topic to real-world complexities can be replicated, as shown in Figure 5.3. This activity is designed to serve as an extension for an integers unit. It shows how accountants' balance sheets, which one might think should simply list gains and losses, instead can also be manipulated in complex ways. This final *dilemma* type of task is not designed for most math-talented students, just those at the end of the continuum who seek out intensely challenging tasks.

Figure 5.3

Integers Extensions

Find the greatest distance among: 5, −2, −9, 11, 15

_____

Are the following statements sometimes, always or never true? Justify your reasoning.

$|X| + X = X$ doubled

$|X| + -X =$ a negative number

If you graph a point X anywhere on a number line, the numbers to the left will always be smaller than X.

_____

Write an equation for:
   A snail climbs 3 feet up a tree, then slips back 2 feet every day. How many days will it take this snail to climb the tree?

_____

Choose among these three:

1. What does 5 look like? Do not use any kind of physical model to explain your answer. What does negative 5 look like? Using physical objects to model your answer, which of these is easier to model?

2. In area problems, if you have a negative measure, you cannot solve the problem. What if you could? What would a rectangle with sides measuring 8 × −2 look like? What would a shoebox with two negative sides look like? Make a drawing and explain your answer.

3. Right now two categories of integers exist: positive and negative. Can you invent a third type of integer? Explain your invention and gives examples of out this new system would work.

_____

Complete the following dilemma on integers in accounting.

Integers in Real Life: Murky Waters

Businesses use integers to show gains and losses and report these to investors who have given their own money to these businesses in order to share in their profits. Obviously it is in the company's interest to show that they are profitable and making money so that they will attract investors.

(Continued)

(Continued)

Unfortunately, in the recent past companies have been able to use complex reporting regulations that allow them to appear more profitable than they actually are.

In the early 2000s, these reporting tricks had allowed companies to claim acquisitions (items they have purchased, so technically losses) as having less value so the losses appear to be less. Similarly, another trick used in the past involved "so-called 'pro-forma' numbers, which strip out negative numbers from a statement." In addition, while tangible costs such as materials must be reported, *intangible* costs can be hidden such as stock options (giving employees the opportunity to purchase company stock in the future at reduced prices) or costs associated with internally developing software computer programs that can increase a company's efficiency. These are more complex to report and can be easily hidden.

Sample Balance Sheet			
Date	**Transaction**	**Price**	**Net Balance**
March 5, 2002	400 air-conditioners*	–$4,000*	$96,000
March 12, 2002	Stock options to employees**	0**	$96,000
March 20, 2002	Marketing research funding (off balance sheet)	–$1,000	$96,000
March 28, 2002	Received 500 air-conditioner filters	–$5,000	$96,000
March 29, 2002	Dorbin to buy air-conditioners*** (to be paid next month)	$10,000***	$106,000
March 30, 2002	Losses we expect to recover	–$20,000	$106,000

*Market value if we resold them—actual price was $250 per air-conditioner.

**This may cost up to $20,000 2 years from now when we actually pay.

***The sale may not actually happen.

Companies report straightforward gains and losses on the main balance sheets, but many of these less tangible type of items could be hidden in footnotes or *off balance sheets,* then suddenly appear on the balance sheets when it suited the company's interests. For example, one off-balance-sheet option, called *special purpose entities,* could be used to fund research and development, or used to hide risks that a company takes. Another trick companies used was to commit to a purchase, but not note that as a debt on their balance sheets, even when they have already taken the material they commit to purchase. Companies could also record gains when they booked a sale, even if the sale never even actually happened.

Hundreds of pages of such loopholes existed that were overly detailed and easy to circumvent, or get around. Formerly, before the 1960s, these rules were simpler, based on broad principles. Yet with the advent of so many lawsuits, accounting firms demanded more detailed, laws to help them in court.

These laws had been designed by organizations that are privately run and staffed by accountants, unlike in Europe where these standards have been set by the government, and the principle of providing a true and fair end balance sheet overrides nitty-gritty rule application. When new regulations are proposed, in the past companies have lobbied and offered cash indirectly to the regulators to force them to act in their favor. The regulators may give in if they need that funding.

Some recommended improvements included having alternate sources, such as the U.S. Treasury, fund the organizations that make these accounting rules so that they won't be so susceptible to donations from companies that want them to make rules in their favor. Other efforts tried internationally have been aimed at preventing off-balance-sheet tricks and forcing companies to disclose more of their less tangible gains or losses, such as forcing companies to write up losses even if they expect to recover them soon, which they previously had not had to do. Such efforts might help, but to avoid the kind of problems of the past, it was argued that companies must "reveal far more economic reality in their accounts than they do at present."

This summary is based on the article "Badly in Need of Repair," which appeared in *The Economist* on May 2, 2002, when accounting problems were popular news items. Since then, further improvements have been made to protect investors from scans. What steps would you have recommended to ensure that businesses balance sheet reporting be more fair and accurate? Respond to the specific obstacles described in this article. Provide at least three recommendations and prioritize which among the three you most recommend and explain why you would prioritize that one.

When designing and evaluating enrichment resources, it can be helpful to keep the following factors in mind:

- Does this activity open out the task and/or allow for multiple-solution possibilities?
- Does it tap abstract thinking capabilities?
- Does it enable students to invent or design novel ways to approach problem-solving?
- Does it allow for flexibility in reasoning?
- Does it allow students to think in greater depth about how and why, not how to?
- Is it inquiry-based?

STRATEGIES TO AVOID

Two strategies that I have frequently seen used, yet that have little research support, are ad hoc peer tutoring and requiring that students master basic skills before tackling higher order thinking challenges. Although carefully planned and well-supported peer-tutoring models, used for limited time and in specific circumstances, have value, regularly asking students to explain topics to peers when they finish early does not offer them the kind of intellectual challenge they need. Also, some students who show extraordinary math talent with higher order thinking can sometimes have difficulty mastering basic facts. As described earlier in this chapter, math talents can manifest in different ways. Students should not be precluded from engaging with higher order math until they have mastered the basic facts. Instead, they should be allowed to master these outside of class through strategies described in the first section of Chapter 3.

IMPORTANCE OF CHALLENGE

It is sometimes believed that students who are high achieving will excel whether or not teachers put much effort into challenging them. This may be true in some cases. Yet research (Tieso, 2005) shows the vast difference good teaching and curriculum can make with these students. This research (Tieso) underscores that if students are not taught at their instructional level, achievement can actually decrease due possibly to the boredom and disengagement that result. Furthermore, often because math has always come so easily to them, they don't develop the strength of perseverance unless they are challenged. They need frequent opportunities to really sink their teeth into solid math challenges so that when they reach higher levels, they will have the inner resources to persevere.

Teachers often find that when they give these students challenges, they frequently, and surprisingly, require teacher assistance, such as scaffolding hints (see www.nrich.org for excellent scaffolding hints provided for each challenge problem). Also, it cannot be assumed that they will always choose the most challenging problems when given the option. Often, they need to be compelled to do so and held to higher standards. To scaffold helping these students persevere more challenging material, they can also be given solutions and taught how to work backward from the answer in these cases. Yet, fundamentally a climate needs to be built over time in which the students are regularly challenged, with coaching and support being given initially. For students who show math talents and are accustomed to coasting easily in math class, it cannot be assumed that they will immediately and easily take to being challenged. Building the skills and how to approach challenges independently with perseverance is a gift we can give them that will have enormous long-term value.

6

Time-Saving Management Strategies

Managing time when making any changes to one's teaching can feel overwhelming. Where should I begin? How much differentiation do I really need to do to maximize the gains for my students? Begin with what makes the most sense and feels most comfortable at first, then slowly extend your efforts over time. This is how I, and the teachers I have worked with, began. We did not try to do everything all at once, yet even with small changes on our part, we immediately saw substantial gains in student achievement. The key to deciding where to begin is figuring out what feels comfortable.

In fact, even teachers working in schools with minimal preparation time found that many changes recommended in this book could be done in time-efficient ways, with exciting gains in student achievement resulting nevertheless. The mantra that these teachers repeatedly quoted to each other was, "Start small with manageable steps, and you will see student achievement rise." The teachers were repeatedly surprised to find that they really did not need to do everything.

Some of the most prominent time-management issues that arise when teachers differentiate mathematics include planning, managing students working on different tasks, assigning homework, and grading. These issues are explored in this chapter.

PLANNING LESSONS AND UNITS

Prioritize Where You Spend Your Time

Time is a finite resource, and so teachers must constantly prioritize how to get the most value for how they spend their time. When making planning decisions, they must constantly ask, "Is the juice worth the squeeze?" Research and our experience shows that practices such as giving detailed feedback or planning tiered lessons that match students' instructional levels significantly raise achievement, even when small changes in these directions are made. Yet, planning tiered lessons takes far less time than does giving detailed feedback to 100-plus students. In optimal circumstances, teachers should do both, but when time doesn't allow for this, teachers need to prioritize and find shortcuts. Ideally, teachers will create a to-do list before starting a unit, evaluate the potential of each item for enhancing achievement and the amount of time each will require, then prioritize which are the best uses of time, keeping in mind the mantra of "start small." Consider the following example.

Ms. Musambee wants to see her students master adding and subtracting fractions as well as enjoy themselves. To achieve this, she debates merely tiering textbook problems (by assigning all or some and challenge problems from one lesson) or having them complete projects from a menu that includes showing their understanding through creating a poster, making a 3-D image, or writing a song. She believes tiering assignments maximizes achievement and that choosing this option requires almost no planning time at all. However, she appreciates the opportunity that posters and songs provide for students to express different learning preferences or multiple intelligences.

She shares this dilemma in a team meeting and finds that the art and music teachers can easily work these kinds of projects into their units, and a colleague shows a briefer, more contained option menu of similar choices that was designed as a homework activity. She appreciates how carefully structured this assignment is and that the teacher who offered it to her had a self scoring rubric so that students could self-evaluate their work (see Figure 6.1). Then, all Ms. Musambee had to do was check the self-scored rubrics to see if she agreed with their scores.

She lamented that she wanted a chance to celebrate different strengths in class, but her colleagues reminded her that how each child approaches tasks varies tremendously and that these differences can be celebrated as well. She used this advice to effortlessly differentiate her next lesson. She decided to observe casually which self-correcting strategies students used to check their work after practicing adding and subtracting fractions. For the following day, she then easily grouped her students by the widely varied methods they used to check their work, which included the following:

1. Those who estimated.

2. Those who used diagrams.

Figure 6.1

Self-Scoring Rubric for a Project

The project I chose was: _____

circle one: poster   3-D image   song/poem

The math that I did not know or had not mastered before doing it was:

_____

_____

_____

_____

As a result of doing the project I learned:

_____

_____

_____

_____

I would score my project on a scale of 1 (not well developed) to 5 (outstanding) as:

Project Presentation: 1   2   3   4   5

List presentation strengths (visual, vocal, literary technique)

_____

_____

_____

(Continued)

(Continued)

Mathematical Content:					
Accuracy:	1	2	3	4	5
Clarity:	1	2	3	4	5

I can prove it is accurate by:

_____

_____

I believe it's clear because:

_____

_____

3. *Those who plugged in the answer to redo the problem.*

4. *Those who redid the problem a second time.*

5 Flexible Student Groups

Fortunately, she had typically high-achieving and low-achieving students mixed in all four groups. Each group was given 5 minutes to write their strategy neatly with markers on poster boards. She then placed the posters on her bulletin board, which she had been wanting to update but had not found the time. This activity tied into the research-validated formative assessment technique of supporting students' efforts to self-check their own work (Sadler & Good, 2006) as well as having students express their individual learning preferences. The subsequent homework project enabled them to express themselves through Gardner's multiple intelligences (see Chapter 3).

Ms. Musambee found a time-efficient compromise in which she identified that her goals were to maximize learning and enjoyment of it and to find a way to celebrate and involve varied learning preferences. To do this, she collaborated across disciplines with colleagues and simplified tasks. To meet her varied goals, she assigned some tasks for homework while reserving high-priority class time for those tasks that would require her assistance and were likely to result in most potent learning. In a nutshell, she began small, with easily manageable choices, and saw her students benefit when she gave the next formative assessment.

Use a Unit and Lesson Planning Checklist

When planning units or lessons, teachers can regularly use the planning checklist shown in Figure 6.2, or design a similar one, suited to their own preferences or needs. Ideally teachers can complete this checklist with colleagues and divide up tasks, as I have done with groups of teachers in schools where I worked. I always find that there is a synergy in these meetings. The teachers agree that generating ideas in groups not only helps divide up the work, but also results in far better quality plans, in the end.

Figure 6.2

Planning Checklist for Unit Differentiation

- Clarify unit *targets* and norms and how you will convey them (e.g., via list/rubric).
- Design/find a *preassessment assessment* for the unit (structure plan for students to self-score it).
- Plan for how you will regularly collect ongoing *formative* assessment to *inform next steps:*
  - Collect homework.
  - Make Formative Assessment sheets I can collect.
  - Have students indicate where they are in their understanding and steps they will take to improve.
- Use assessment data and coplan next steps for how to *tier lessons* (challenges and supports) to run different activities at the same time with students in groups.
- Create options for d*ifferentiating challenge and support* in the unit with the following:
  - Challenge packets.
  - Support for low achieving (sheets, research on Internet, common misunderstandings).
- Create tiered homework, quizzes, and tests.
  - Tips for prioritizing which of the above gives the most *bang for the buck.*
  - Do a quick 15-minute scan of teachers' editions and the Internet for ideas/tasks for tiers. Set a timer to make sure that you do not go over 15 minutes.
  - Begin with small, manageable tiers—just draft or find a challenge list to begin.
  - Convey targets through preassessments—or just in a handout that students reference regularly.
  - Strive to keep students on the same topic, but if crunched for time, it is better to offer unrelated challenges than to have some kids do work that is too easy that bores them.

This planning checklist is not intended to be an exhaustive to-do list that should be done for every unit. Again, using just a few will lift student achievement. All need not be done to achieve these gains. In fact, the ideas in this checklist cannot take place in every lesson, nor should they. For example, at times, whole group lessons in the same tasks for all are necessary.

Cut Scoring Time by Designing Feedback Systems

Teachers can further guard their time by having students frequently self-score their own work with answer keys, particularly given the research that shows how valuable this is for students (Hattie & Timperley, 2007). Creating answer keys can take time, but the work can be shared by several teachers, done by a parent volunteer, or done on a smart board while teaching, then saved for future years.

When teachers do score work, they can easily create structured ways to give advising feedback to one problem per page and merely score all other problems as correct/incorrect. Although it is ideal to provide extensive comments throughout, this is not always feasible or necessary. Giving some detailed feedback can benefit students. For example, Figure 6.3 shows a shortened version of teacher feedback given on a formative assessment activity midway through a unit on multiplying fractions. The sheet had 10 problems. Ms. Musambee gave all 10 answers in a key after they finished. Ms. Musambee chose one that seemed representative of typical errors for more detailed feedback. Students then copied incorrect problems, corrected them according to the model, and self-analyzed what went wrong with each using the structured checklist given. Detailed feedback is immensely helpful, and through such a structured system, students are able to get it. After Ms. Musambee gave this, she found it cut her scoring time dramatically. She also felt students were getting equally valuable, if not even more valuable, quality feedback than she would have given if she had sacrificed her entire evening providing individualized feedback to each student. Time-saving strategies like these are what make using formative assessment to differentiate instruction feasible.

Figure 6.3

Structured Feedback Format

For students with two or more errors

After you have used an answer key to score all problems, please look more closely at up to two problems that you had difficulty with. Copy them here, using the sample and the checklist to help you work out the correct answer, and check off each difficulty you've had.

Sample Corrected Problem:

1. $2\frac{5}{6} \times 1\frac{3}{4} =$

$$\frac{17}{6} \times \frac{7}{4} =$$

$$\frac{119}{24} =$$

$$4\frac{23}{24} =$$

Copy an incorrect and corrected version of one you got wrong here:

Check off errors you made:

- ❏ Made a simple basic fact error when converting.
- ❏ Forgot to convert mixed number to improper fraction.
- ❏ Forgot to multiply across.
- ❏ Forgot to convert back to mixed number.
- ❏ Other (explain): _____.

Have Students Condense Reflections

When students do lengthier self-reflections on tests they took or other tasks, they can be asked to do three of them before condensing them into one brief two- to three-sentence overview that they then turn into the teacher. This has tremendous value in helping them hone and clarify their thinking as well as also dramatically cutting teacher scoring time. When writing justifications, they could self-score them with rubrics, such as the one provided in Chapter 2 (refer to Figure 2.14), then redo them and turn them in with a brief condensed summary of improvements made from one draft to the next. Not only does this save teacher time, it also allows students to benefit from the deep processing needed to reflect on the contents of the rubric. One student I worked with had become extremely passive and withdrawn. After she began self-scoring her own work, condensing reflections on her work and learning processes, she came alive. In taking charge of her own learning, she found more purpose, enjoyed class more, and took such pride in her improvements. Since self-directedness is integral to differentiated instruction, sharing scoring of work enables teachers to redistribute their workload when they begin differentiating, rather than differentiating resulting in a sharp increase in teachers work load.

Find Extra Time

When running workshops on differentiating math instruction, I am frequently asked where teachers find the time for the additional planning and scoring of formative assessments. When actually planning for tiered or differentiated lesson, teachers can use textbooks that provide tiered tasks or draw from the many resources listed in Chapter 3. These lessons should be saved for future access ideally in well-organized electronic folders or in carefully labeled and organized paper folders.

Teachers often worry that differentiation means planning three different lessons. This has not been our experience. The time it takes to plan tiers or different activities can be minimal, when for example, mere structural changes are made—such as some groups using manipulatives and others not, or some working on a specific investigation while others complete a practice set that they feel they need to do to be comfortable with a particular concept. In my experience, I have actually never planned three separate lessons, and so I feel this is one of the biggest myths of differentiation. Ensuring one has challenges ready and some ways to offer support on hand is a great start.

MANAGING STUDENTS WORKING ON DIFFERENT TASKS

Another piece to differentiating instruction is planning for and managing students working on different tasks. Teachers who have ample experience doing this can skim or skip this section. Teachers frequently share that when reviewing a thorny homework or class work problem, they often determine that part of the class needs more review, while some are bored and ready to move on. When confronted with this dilemma unexpectedly, for example, while reviewing the previous night's homework, teachers can have some students move on to continue ahead with the day's lesson, or to work on the challenges posted in the room or in assignment packets. Any differentiation, even small steps, is superior to students not working at their instructional levels.

Form and Run Flexible Groups

Flexible groups are common practices in any differentiated class. Teachers can use extremely simple and manageable ways to form and run these.  By flexible, this means that group configurations should regularly change, based on preassessment results and how these are used to design group configurations. Admittedly, certain students will regularly be working at higher readiness levels, but each student should be given a fresh chance to be in any group after each preassessment.

Students will work in groups usually for only part of the lesson, and groups need not be formed every day. After the lesson is launched, research shows students benefit from time spent working with peers who are at similar readiness levels (Tieso, 2005). In this way, teachers can more easily meet their instructional needs. Flexible groups are not cooperative learning or tracked groups. Cooperative learning groups frequently use heterogeneous groupings. These kinds of groupings are appropriate when students have no knowledge of the mathematical concept, as in the case when they are all learning about expected value for the first time. Tracked groups are formed once at the start of the year and inflexibly maintained all year, for the most part. In contrast, flexible groups are formed and can change after each preassessment.

When different tasks are occurring in a classroom, inevitably there is more bustle to be contained. Students need coaching to do the following:

5 Flexible Student Groups

- *Use the most time- and space-efficient ways to get into groups.* Getting students into groups should be done efficiently. As noted, some teachers spontaneously group mid-lesson. Students should not move desks, but should move themselves to designated areas. If a teacher has planned with groups in mind, she or he can display group categories on the board and arrange magnetic cards with student names on them among the categories, or label pocket charts and place student name cards in the appropriate pockets. Then these groups can be formed very easily, often without much planning beforehand at all.
- *Use "10-inch voices" to keep the noise levels down.*
- *Respond to signals for quiet, such as a gong, chime, or soft bell, or raise two fingers and stop speaking.*
- *Ask three before me.* This means asking three peers for help before going to the teacher.
- *Write out questions.* We have found that having students write their questions and submit them to the teacher while she is running another group of students is less disruptive. Some students can actually often answer the question once they have clearly articulated it, so frequently they do not even need to ask it once they have finished writing it. If a student is seeking teacher attention, this disrupts their strategy. However, if they do use the strategy and therefore do not disturb the teacher, do be sure to give the child special attention for having been so thoughtful about not disturbing the teacher while working with a group, particularly if that child is seeking attention. A sample format for students to write out questions is shown in Figure 6.4. Again, this is an excellent way to save time. Interruptions add up and can result in small group actual instruction time being cut in half.

Figure 6.4

Sheet for Writing Out Questions

The question I have is:

_____

_____

_____

_____

_____

(Continued)

(Continued)

The parts of the problem I understand are:

_____

_____

_____

_____

_____

In an effort to answer this question myself, I have:

– checked with a peer

– reviewed alternate text explanations

– searched on the Internet

- *Follow rules and directions for the assigned task.* Clearly stated directions should be given to each group and a summary of them posted. For complex tasks, direction cards can be given as in the example for area and volume of cylinders shown in Figure 6.5. This lesson is an extension to follow a lesson in which students have mastered the volume of cylinders. (Note the reason for the answer to the question in Step 5: the surface area of the circles on the top and bottom changes size and that affects the total volume.)

Provide for Additional Independent Work

If students complete work early, there should be abundant extensions or challenges available that they can work on. For example, one teacher had a notebook full of copies of related extensions that students would choose from and complete if they finished early. Using preassessments or current lists of which targets a student has mastered within a given unit, students should determine which activities they need to complete.

Projected time needed for each activity in a booklet like this should be noted in the upper corner of the activity so that if students have only 10 minutes, they can choose accordingly. In addition, teachers can post weekly challenges in the room that are tied to the current unit topic, and students can work on these if they finish early. Learning centers can also be created in corners of the classroom that students can go to if they finish work early.

Establish Learning Centers

Running centers offers an ideal opportunity to differentiate instruction. At the simplest level, students can simply be working on different tasks in

Figure 6.5

Unit: Surface Area and Volume of Cylinders

Activity: Finding the volume of cylinders with same lateral surface area but different configurations.

Materials: 2 pieces of transparency paper, tape, plastic rice or some small objects, and a rubber surface. (Given hunger issues in the world, I recommend not using real food.)

Prediction: In your math notebooks, write out a prediction: What happens to the volume of a cylinder if the surface area remains the same but the shape of the cylinder changes?

Steps:

1. Using transparency paper, roll it lengthwise into a tall, slim roll and tape the edges where they meet so that it will close.

2. Again using same size transparency paper, roll it widthwise so that a thicker but shorter cylinder is created—tape the edges so that it will close.

3. Fill the first taller cylinder with plastic rice.

4. Then pour that same plastic rice into the second thicker cylinder.

5. Although the same paper was used to build both cylinders, do they hold the same amount?

Reflection: Write out the formula for finding the volume of a cylinder that you learned last week (check text for the formula). Then, with the formula in mind, reflect on the reason for your answer to the question in Step 5.

four different areas of the room. These centers could have laminated work cards with directions for activities students can complete when they have finished assignments. All of the materials students need for these activities should be stored right in the learning centers so that they do not need to move around the classroom. Ideally, no more than four students should be at a center at one time. To keep centers small, some students can do desk activities while waiting for a turn at the center because running more than four centers can become logistically overwhelming.

Centers do not need to require excessive planning. In fact, they can actually save planning time. It usually takes students several days to do all the activities in the centers. So teachers are freed up from planning for those days, after the initial planning and set up is done. Teachers can also share planning for the centers, dividing up the work and running them on different days. I have seen this work well in schools, and teachers have saved tremendous planning time, as a result.

The tasks at all four centers should focus on the same concept. For example, when teaching that the angles inside a triangle equal 180°, students could rotate through four centers working on varied tasks. The first task might be measuring the three angles inside of six different triangles with a protractor. The second might be cutting out a triangle, then tearing off the three corners and lining them up to form a straight line. The third might be cutting out a triangle then folding in the angles toward the middle to again form a straight line. The last center might have a challenge such as creating a triangle and seeing what happens when the angles inside measure more or less than 180°.

Teach Specific Self-Directed Routines

Another specific way to prepare students to maximize the effectiveness of their independent work time and avoid getting stuck on problems is the researched-based MATH strategy (Hock, Pulvers, Deshler, & Schumaker, 2001). The steps can also be posted in the classroom and referred to as needed (see Figure 6.6).

Figure 6.6

The MATH Strategy

1. **M**ap out or determine what needs to be solved.

2. **A**nalyze the problem by comparing it with model problems in the textbook.

3. **T**ake action to solve the problem.

4. **H**ave a look back to check the answer.

ASSIGNING HOMEWORK

Plan and Collect Homework in Chunks

Teachers can use carefully organized plans to minimize the additional workload of differentiating homework. As an example, following the preassessments, teachers can design two or three sets of homework plans for each week and put them on a one-page handout (see Figure 6.7) so that they don't need to attend to homework all week. Homework can be collected in packets weekly rather than submitted daily since students are self-scoring it. Challenges can be made available to all, but only be required of some, as Figure 6.7 illustrates. When differentiating homework, it is essential to convey that all assigned homework for each group is required, particularly challenges.

Of course, homework plans can change midweek so these plans should be flexible and students should be accustomed to noting switches or changes teachers make to them midweek. Sound like a long weekend? Not the case! The teachers I know who use the system keep an eye on homework all week, answering questions and glancing over it. Also, students have been self-scoring it all week so there is no scoring to be done—just checking to make sure it was accurately scored and complete. Also, students write a condensed two to three line summary on the top of

Figure 6.7

Weekly Homework Packets

Please turn in this week's homework on Friday. All homework should be self-corrected, with notes on what you learned from each error and steps you'll take to avoid it in the future.

Monday:

Problem set numbers ___–___ on p. _____.

Challenges #_____ in extension packet.

Tuesday:

Problem set numbers ___–___ on p. _____.

Challenges #_____ in extension packet.

Wednesday:

Problem set numbers ___–___ on p. _____.

Challenges #_____ in extension packet.

Thursday:

Problem set numbers ___–___ on p. _____.

Challenges #_____ in extension packet.

If your preassessment was nearly perfect, you must do the optional challenges. You are to select three of the most challenging problems in each standard problem set also. Of course, you are welcome to do the challenges even if you had difficulty with the preassessment.

the homework packet, in which they reflect on any problems/questions they had and how they addressed them. Doing this, we have found, actually gives us the most powerful sense of where they are at, and being written so concisely, is a quick read for the teacher. Other options certainly exist and can be equally helpful. The key is having students self score their work as this is both extremely well supported by the research and dramatically saves teacher time.

Encourage Student-Directed Differentiation

Students can also be encouraged to propose ways to compact or extend their homework, based on where they are in mastering the unit's listed targets. This can be challenging for kids to do well, though it is an ideal way to foster self-directedness and save teacher planning time. As an example, in a unit on probability one child who'd scored 96% on the preassessments was stumped by one type of problem—identifying the difference between a permutation and a combination. His teacher often reminded her students that he has found students typically need to do about 24 practice problems with at least 80% accuracy to master a topic. Although this student had tested out of most of the homework because of his high preassessments score, he chose to do 24 practice problems that required him to determine whether the problem was a permutation or a combination in order to master this topic.

Differentiate Homework

If a teacher has assigned homework for the class and feels that several students have mastered the topic during the class lesson despite having not shown mastery of it on the preassessment, she or he can have them star just those challenge problems that they should do. If a student needs extra practice with certain skills such as multiplication, Internet sites can be recommended, and they can keep a log of time spent in extra practice as described in Chapter 2 (refer to Figure 2.4).

Involve Students in Correcting Homework

Tiered tasks with the same answer, but varied levels of support, such as embedded hints or more steps provided, are ideal for homework because the whole class can correct it together. Having students self-correct homework in advance while they are at home saves time that can then be used to review two sets of questions on different homework the next day in class. Students can use self-correcting tasks, such as riddles; or teachers can send home or post answers on a website. Students can also be given answer keys in class to correct their own homework.

On days when all the homework is not the same, students should not have to sit through corrections of homework that they did not do when it is below their instructional level. They can work ahead in challenge packets instead, while the teacher answers questions from the other group. Also students can discuss homework questions with peers first, as the teacher rotates between groups answering questions. Keep in mind that running more than two homework groups can be logistically challenging.

Differentiate Support for Students Who Don't Turn in Homework

If students don't turn in homework, they can be asked to complete a time-management form in which they list out how they spend their time as well as create a time-management strategy. If they don't understand it, they can fill out a checklist of efforts made so that they and their teacher can assess the problem and find an individualized solution (see Figure 6.8).

To further differentiate support, if students have general difficulty despite these efforts, a parent can be asked to send a weekly email or note in the study/homework book as to whether homework has been completed. One teacher with a student whose parents had organizational challenges and forget to send the email weekly found that this student's grandfather was better at doing this. Asking parents to initiate a weekly check-in is just realistic in a time-management sense, as teachers with 100-plus students cannot easily stay on top of initiating emails regularly for missing homework. Time spent finding how to get parents to check in (e.g., have the grandparent do it) will save teachers inordinate amounts of time down the road.

Figure 6.8

Why I Didn't Do My Homework

If you did not understand the homework problems, explain why for EVERY problem. Explain what you did understand and exactly where you got stuck. Do this for each problem.

Answer this question by selecting one of the choices below:

What efforts did you make to complete the homework?

- I called a friend from class.
- I typed in key words into Internet math-help sites or Google.
- I reread directions carefully, rewrote them in my own words, and highlighted 2–3 important words in them and looked back at prior examples in the book.
- I checked an alternative math book for another explanation.
- I asked an adult for help.
- I reviewed my notes from class.
- I rewrote the examples from the book and reread the chapter carefully.

GRADING

Ideally, grading should be minimized in formative assessment models. Research actually shows that grading can undermine learning (Black & Wiliam, 1998). Grading, when required, needs to convey as analytically as possible where a student is in relation to mastering expected standards. Therefore, when teachers must grade, it can be done in ways that serve as powerful feedback that should be understandable to students. For example, a B on a test tells little, but an analytic checklist of mastered and unmastered concepts on the test is far more helpful than a single grade, even if the students fill out the checklist themselves.

Students should not be graded on certain primarily formative assessment such as preassessments or homework that was practice at achieving standards, though homework effort should be shown in an effort grade, separate from a grade for mastery and standards. Also, teachers need not grade everything students submit. However, students should self-score preassessments and be given the option of redoing a closely similar quiz so that they can see their progress. A retake could count as part of the class participation grade or as a weighted homework grade. Because of how students did on the preassessments and formative assessment along the way during the unit, teachers may choose to create a slightly more challenging test or to add bonus questions to a test. These can be required of certain students. If students take a more challenging test and score a slightly lower grade, the teacher could weight that grade differently when calculating the final scores. If the unit standards covered on the tests were all mastered and only the bonuses were missed, then that can be taken into consideration when teachers are figuring out the final grade for the course. Similarly, students who attempt more challenging tasks can be marked up if they have mastered the class standard and only struggled with elements of the task that were higher than the standard.

More specifically, if students are expected to master certain unit standards, teachers should put all of these on the unit assessment. Students who attempted challenges that go beyond the standards can get extra credit toward homework and class participation grades. If the bonus requires mastery of the test standards, then it can count as a retake might, in that its credit can replace lost credit on either items on the test that were incorrect—only if it does in fact show that the student had mastered standards in an alternate context or problem. Bonus points or extra credit should not enable students to bypass mastering standards.

WRAP UP

At the start of this book, you took a differentiation self-assessment. Now that you've finished the book and begun using some of these practices, you can retake it (see Figure 6.9) and celebrate your own growth in using *Formative Assessment to Differentiate Math Instruction.*

Figure 6.9

Teacher Self-Assessment

Differentiating Math Practices Rubric

We all begin in different places and pursue different goals as we grow as teachers. This self-assessment provides an overview of practices, not a required list, that can enhance your skills at using formative assessment to differentiate instruction.

On a scale of 1–4, rate how frequently you do each practice:

1—I do this often,   2—occasionally,   3—have tried it,   4—haven't tried this yet

Convey Norms and Targets				
1. I foster self-directed, independent approaches to learning.	1	2	3	4
2. I emphasize to students that doing different work helps everyone get what he or she needs.	1	2	3	4
3. I clearly convey objectives (targets) before each unit.	1	2	3	4
Assessment				
4. I use diagnostic preassessment tasks before each unit.	1	2	3	4
5. I systematically collect informal and formal assessment data all along.	1	2	3	4
Coplan Next Steps				
6. I use assessment data to tier homework, class activities, and assessments.	1	2	3	4
7. I have students self-score assessments and use the results to decide next steps to take.	1	2	3	4
8. I stress the importance of self-initiated student learning, based on teacher feedback and self-scored assessments.	1	2	3	4
Grouping and Tiering				
9. I regularly use flexible groupings (often 3) for differentiated tasks.	1	2	3	4
10. Based on my review of homework and/or class participation during instruction, I enable those students who indicate mastery to move on as I assist others.	1	2	3	4
11. I draw on supplemental resources (alternate texts, websites) for differentiated activities.	1	2	3	4
Challenge and Support				
12. I select from my own bank of strategies for filling in calculation gaps, solidifying procedural steps, and clarifying concepts.	1	2	3	4
13. I select from my own bank of strategies for challenging students such as open-ended tasks, higher order questions, abstract projects, projects compacting contracts, and extension resources.	1	2	3	4
Homework and Graded Assessments				
14. I differentiate homework and assessments and hold students accountable for the different work they do.	1	2	3	4

When Ms. Musambee and Mr. Martin began differentiating instruction, they were initially surprised to discover how much they already do. In one telling moment, when they were showing each other their systems for differentiating homework and some differentiated class tasks, Ms. Musambee cheerfully observed, "Wow, we already do a lot of differentiating!" This is true for most conscientious teachers. Differentiating comes naturally as we respond to the perceived unique learning needs of the individuals sitting in front of us, depending on us to help them use their time to get the most learning out of the work they do. This book is an effort to enhance the effectiveness of these efforts.

Suggested Resources

Andreescu, T., & Gelca, R. (2008). *Mathematical Olympiad challenges* (2nd ed.). Boston, MA: Birkhauser Boston.

Balka, D. S. (2001). *Exploring geometry with geofix.* Rowley, MA: Didax Educational Resources.

Doyle, D., Ellis, M., Friel, S. N., Mygard, C., Pugalee, D., & Rachlin, S. (2001). *Navigating through algebra in grades 6–8 (principles and standards for school mathematics navigations series)* (Pap/Cdr ed.). Reston, VA: National Council of Teachers of Mathematics.

Espeland, P., & Winebrenner, S. (2001). *Teaching gifted kids in the regular classroom: strategies and techniques every teacher can use to meet the academic needs of the gifted and talented* (Rev. updated ed.). Minneapolis, MN: Free Spirit Publishing.

Hope, J., Leutzinger, L., Reys, B., & Reys, R. (1988). *Mental math in the primary grades.* New York, NY: Dale Seymour Publications.

Husted, T. (2003). *Higher-order thinking, reading, writing in mathematics (Math detective).* Pacific Grove, CA: Critical Thinking Books & Software.

Jitendra, A. K. (2007). *Solving math word problems: Teaching students with learning disabilities using schema-based instruction.* Austin, TX: PRO-ED.

Marcy, S., & Marcy, J. (1989). *Middle school math with pizzazz.* Ventura, CA: Creative Publications, Division of Educational Publishing Corporation.

Opie, B. (1996). *Masterminds riddle math series pre-algebra: Reproducible skill builders and higher order thinking activities based on NCTM standards* (Some pages penciled ed.). Nashville, TN: Incentive.

Woodward, J., & Stroh, M. (2004). *Subtraction computational skills practice fact fluency and more.* Longmont, CO: Sopris West.

Woodward, J., & Stroh, M. (2004). *Addition computational skills practice fact fluency and more.* Longmont, CO: Sopris West.

Zaccaro, E. (2005). *Challenge math (for the elementary and middle school student* (2nd ed.). Dubuque, IA: Hickory Grove Press.

Online Resources

BrainBashers: Puzzles and Brain Teasers: http://www.brainbashers.com

ETA/Cuisenaire: Hands-On Manipulatives and Supplemental Educational Materials for Grades PreK–12, soft 100, 10, and 1 cm squares, algebra tiles, geometric solids: http://www.etacuisenaire.com

Learning Resources—Educational Toys and Hands-On Learning Materials for Classrooms: http://www.Learningresources.com

Math Practice and Math Help with MathScore—Free Practice Worksheets and Demos: http://www.mathscore.com

References

Andrade, H. (2010). Students as the definitive source of formative assessment: Academic self-assessment and the self-regulation of learning. In H. Andrade & G. Cizek (Eds.), *Handbook of formative assessment* (pp. 90–105). New York, NY: Routledge.

Black P., & Wiliam, D. (1998). Inside the black box: Raising standards through classroom assessment. *Phi Delta Kappan, 80*(2), 139–148.

Black, P., Harrison, C., Lee, C., Marshall, B., & Wiliam, D. (2003). *Assessment for Learning. Putting it into practice.* Maidenhead, Berkshire: Open University Press.

Bulkley, K., Nabors Oláh, L., & Blanc, S. (2010). Introduction to the special issue on "Benchmarks for success? Interim assessment as a strategy for educational improvement." *Peabody Journal of Education: Issues of Leadership, Policy, and Organizations, 85*(2), 115–124.

Day, R. Frey, P., Howard, A., Molix-Bailey, R., Ott, J., Pelfrey, R., Hutchens, D., . . . Willard, T. (2009). *Math connects: Concepts, skills, and problem solving.* Glencoe, IL: McGraw Hill.

Delazer, M., Domahs, F., Bartha, L., Brenneis, C., Lochy, A., Trieb. T., & Benke, T. (2003). Learning complex arithmetic—A fMRI study. *Cognitive Brain Research, 18,* 76–88.

Dienes, Z. (2000). Unifying consciousness with explicit knowledge. *Consciousness and Cognition, 9,* S32.

Dorn, S. (2010). The political dilemmas of formative assessment. *Exceptional Children, 76* (3), 325–337.

Elawar, M. C., & Corno, L. (1985). A factorial experiment in teachers' written feedback on student homework: Changing teacher behaviour a little rather than a lot. *Journal of Educational Psychology, 77,* 162–173.

Ellis, E. S., & Lenz, B. K. (1996). Perspectives on instruction in learning strategies. In D. D. Deshler, E. S. Ellis, & B. K. Lenz (Eds.), *Teaching adolescents with learning disabilities* (pp. 9–60). Denver, CO: Love Publishing.

Foegen, A., & Morrison, C. (2010). Putting algebra progress monitoring into practice: Insights from the field. *Intervention in School and Clinic, 46*(2), 95–103.

Foegen, A., Olson, J. R., & Impecoven-Lind, L. (2008). Developing progress monitoring measures for secondary mathematics: An illustration in algebra. *Assessment for Effective Intervention, 33,* 240–249.

Fosnot, C. T., & Dolk, M. (2001). *Young mathematicians at work: Constructing multiplication and division.* Portsmouth, NH: Heinemann Press.

Fuchs, L., & Fuchs, D. (1986). Effects of systematic formative evaluation: A meta-analysis. *Exceptional Children, 53*(3), 199–208.

Gardner, H. (1983). *Frames of mind.* New York, NY: Basic Books.

Gersten, R., Beckmann, S., Clarke, B., Foegen, A., Marsh, L., Star, J. R., & Witzel, B. (2009). *Assisting students struggling with mathematics: Response to Intervention (RtI) for elementary and middle schools* (NCEE 2009-4060). Washington, DC:

National Center for Education Evaluation and Regional Assistance, Institute of Education Sciences, U.S. Department of Education. Retrieved December 22, 2010, from http://ies.ed.gov/ncee/wwc/pdf/practiceguides/rti_math_pg_042109.pdf

Gersten, R., & Chard, D. (1999). Number sense: Rethinking mathematics instruction for students with mathematical disabilities. *Journal of Special Education, 33,* 19–28.

Gersten, R., Chard, D. J., Jayanthi, M., Baker, S. K., Morphy, P., & Flojo, J. (2009). Mathematics instruction for students with learning disabilities: A meta-analysis of instructional components. *Review of Educational Research, 79*(3), 1202–1242.

Ginsburg, H. (2009). The challenge of formative assessment in mathematics education: Children's minds, teachers' minds. *Human Development, 52,* 109–128.

Greenes, C. (1981). Identifying the gifted student in mathematics. *Arithmetic Teacher, 28,* 14–18.

Hattie, J., & Timperley, H. (2007). The power of feedback. *Review of Education Research, 77,* 81–112.

Heacox, D. (2002*). Differentiating instruction in the regular classroom: How to reach and teach all learners, grades 3–12.* Minneapolis, MN: Free Spirit.

Hegarty, M., & Kozhevnikov, M. (1999). Types of visual-spatial representations and mathematical problem solving. *Journal of Educational Psychology, 91,* 684–689.

Heritage, M. (2008). *Learning progressions: Supporting instruction and formative assessment.* Paper prepared for the Formative Assessment for Teachers and Students (FAST) State Collaborative on Assessment and Student Standards (SCASS) of the Council of Chief State School Officers (CCSSO), Washington, DC.

Heritage, H. M., & Niemi, D. (2006). Toward a framework for using student mathematical representations as formative assessments. *Educational Assessment, 11,* 265–282.

Heubner, T (2010). Differentiating instruction. *Educational Leadership, 67*(5), 79–81.

Hock, M. F., Pulvers, K. A., Deshler, D. D., & Schumaker, J. B. (2001). The effects of an after-school tutoring program on the academic performance of at-risk students and students with LD. *Remedial and Special Education, 22*(3), 172–186.

Hudson, P., & Miller, S. P. (2006). *Designing and implementing mathematics instruction for students with diverse learning needs.* Boston, MA: Allyn & Bacon.

Ives, B. (2007). Graphic organizers applied to secondary algebra instruction for students with learning disorders. *Learning Disabilities Research & Practice, 22*(2), 110–118.

Jitendra, A. K. (2002). Teaching students math problem-solving through graphic representations. *Teaching Exceptional Children, 34*(4), 34–38.

Krätzig, G. P., & Arbuthnott, K. D. (2006). Perceptual learning style and learning proficiency: A test of the hypothesis. *Journal of Educational Psychology, 98*(1), 238–246.

Lappan, G., Fey, J., Fitzgerald, W., Friel, S., & Phillips, E. (2006). *Connected Mathematics Program 2.* Needham, MA: Pearson Prentice Hall.

Levine, M. (1994). *Educational care: A system for understanding and helping children with learning problems at home and in school.* Cambridge, MA: Educators Publishing Service.

Marshall, S. P. (1995). *Schemas in problem solving.* New York, NY: Cambridge University Press.

Mercer, C. D., & Mercer, A. R. (1993). *Teaching students with learning problems* (4th ed.). New York, NY: Macmillan Publishing.

Miller, S. P., & Hudson, P. J. (2007). Using evidence based practices to build mathematics competence related to conceptual, procedural, and declarative knowledge. *Learning Disabilities Research and Practice, 22,* 47–57.

Montague, M. (2007). Self-regulation and mathematics instruction. *Learning Disabilities Research & Practice, 22*(1), 75–83.

Murray, M., & Jorgensen, J. (2007). *The differentiated math classroom: A guide for teachers, K–8.* Heinneman Publishing.

National Council of Teachers of Mathematics (NCTM). (2000). *Principles and standards for school mathematics.* Reston, VA: Author.

Newstead, K., & Murray, H. (1998). Young students' constructions of fractions. In A. Olivier & K. Newstead (Eds.), *Proceedings of the 22nd Conference of the International Group for the Psychology of Mathematics Education,* 3 (pp. 295–302). Stellenbosch, South Africa.

Oláh, L. N., Lawrence, N. R., & Riggan, M. (2010). Learning to learn from benchmark assessment data: How teachers analyze results. *Peabody Journal of Education, 85*(2), 226–245.

Reeves, T. C. (2000) Alternative assessment approaches for online learning environments in higher education. *Higher Education Journal of Educational Computing Research, 23,* 101–111.

Riccomini, P. J. & Witzel, B. S. (2010a). *Solving equations.* Upper Saddle River, NJ: Pearson Education.

Riccomini, P. J. & Witzel, B. S. (2010b). *Response to intervention in math.* Thousand Oaks, CA: Corwin.

Sadler, P., & Good, E. (2006). The impact of self- and peer-grading on student learning. *Educational Assessment, 11*(1), 1–31.

Sak, U. (2009). Test of the three-mathematical minds (M3) for the identification of mathematically gifted students. *Roeper Review, 31,* 53–67.

Sanjay, R. (2002). A new approach to an old order. *Mathematics Teaching in the Middle School, 8*(4), 193–195.

Scherer, M. (2006). Celebrate strengths, nurture affinities: A conversation with Mel Levine. *Educational Leadership, 64*(1), 8–15.

Small, M. (2010). *More good questions: Great ways to differentiate secondary instruction.* New York, NY: Teachers College Press, National Council of Teachers of Mathematics, Nelson Education.

Stading, M., Williams, R. L., & McLaughlin, T. F. (1996). Improving academic performance through self-management: Cover, copy, and compare. *Intervention in School and Clinic, 32*(2), 113–118.

Stecker, P. M., Fuchs, L. S., & Fuchs, D. (2005). Using curriculum-based measurement to improve student achievement: Review of research. *Psychology in the Schools, 42,* 795–820.

Swanson, H. L., & Deshler, D. D. (2003). Instructing adolescents with disabilities: Converting a meta-analysis to practice. *Journal of Learning Disabilities, 36*(2), 124–135.

Test, D. W., & Ellis, M. F. (2005). The effects of LAP fractions on addition and subtraction of fractions with students with mild disabilities. *Education and Treatment of Children, 28*(1), 11–24.

Tieso, C. (2005). The effects of grouping practices and curricular adjustments on achievement. *Journal for the Education of the Gifted, 29*(1), 60–89.

Tindal, G., & Ketterlin-Geller, L. (2004). *Research on mathematics test accommodations relevant to NAEP testing.* Washington, DC: National Assessment Governing Board.

Tomlinson, C. (1999). *The differentiated classroom: Responding to the needs of all learners.* Alexandria, VA: Association for Supervision and Curriculum.

Van Garderen, D. (2006). Spatial visualization, visual imagery, and mathematical problem solving of students with varying abilities. *Journal of Learning Disabilities, 39,* 496–506.

Wiggins, G. (1998). *Educative assessment: Designing assessments to inform and improve student performance.* San Francisco, CA: Jossey-Bass.

Wiggins, G., & McTighe, J. (2005). *Understanding by design* (Expanded 2nd ed.). Alexandria, VA: Association for Supervision and Curriculum Development.

Wiliam, D. (2010). An integrative summary of the research literature. In H. L. Andrade & G. J. Cizek (Eds.), *Handbook of formative assessment* (pp. 18–40). New York, NY: Routledge.

Winebrenner, S. (2001). *Teaching gifted kids in the regular classroom.* Minneapolis, MN: Free Spirit Publishing.

Witzel, B. S. (2005). Using CRA to teach Algebra to students with math difficulties in inclusive settings. *Learning Disabilities: A Contemporary Journal, 3*(2), 49–60.

Witzel, B. S., Mercer, C. D., & Miller, M. D. (2003). Teaching algebra to students with learning difficulties: An investigation of an explicit instruction model. *Learning Disabilities Research & Practice, 18*(2), 121–131.

Woodward, J. (2006). Developing automaticity in multiplication facts: Integrating strategy instruction with timed practice drills. *Learning Disability Quarterly, 29,* 269–289.

Woodward, J., & Stroh, M. (2004). *Transitional mathematics program.* Longmont, CO: Sopris West.

Xin, Y. P. (2007). Word-problem-solving tasks presented in textbooks and their relation to student performance: A cross-curriculum comparison case study. *The Journal of Educational Research, 100,* 347–359.

Xin, Y. P., & Jitendra, A. K. (2006). Teaching problem solving skills to middle school students with mathematics difficulties: Schema-based strategy instruction. In M. Montague & A. K. Jitendra (Eds.), *Teaching mathematics to middle school students with learning difficulties* (pp. 51–71). New York, NY: Guilford Press.

Xin, Y. P., Jitendra, A., & Deatline-Buchman, A. (2005). Effects of mathematical word problem-solving instruction on middle school students with learning problems. *The Journal of Special Education, 39,* 181–192.

Ysseldyke, J., & Tardrew, S. (2007). Use of a progress monitoring system to enable teachers to differentiate mathematics instruction. *Journal of Applied School Psychology, 24*(1), 1–28.

Zrebiec Uberti, H., Mastropieri, M., & Scruggs, T. (2004). Check it off: Individualizing a math algorithm for students with disabilities via self-monitoring checklists. *Intervention in School and Clinic, 39*(5), 269–275.

Index

CORWIN
A SAGE Company

The Corwin logo—a raven striding across an open book—represents the union of courage and learning. Corwin is committed to improving education for all learners by publishing books and other professional development resources for those serving the field of PreK–12 education. By providing practical, hands-on materials, Corwin continues to carry out the promise of its motto: **"Helping Educators Do Their Work Better."**

NATIONAL COUNCIL OF
TEACHERS OF MATHEMATICS

The National Council of Teachers of Mathematics is a public voice of mathematics education, supporting teachers to ensure equitable mathematics learning of the highest quality for all students through vision, leadership, professional development, and research.